1,000,000 Books

are available to read at

www.ForgottenBooks.com

Read online
Download PDF
Purchase in print

ISBN 978-1-333-34992-9
PIBN 10493846

This book is a reproduction of an important historical work. Forgotten Books uses state-of-the-art technology to digitally reconstruct the work, preserving the original format whilst repairing imperfections present in the aged copy. In rare cases, an imperfection in the original, such as a blemish or missing page, may be replicated in our edition. We do, however, repair the vast majority of imperfections successfully; any imperfections that remain are intentionally left to preserve the state of such historical works.

Forgotten Books is a registered trademark of FB &c Ltd.
Copyright © 2018 FB &c Ltd.
FB &c Ltd, Dalton House, 60 Windsor Avenue, London, SW19 2RR.
Company number 08720141. Registered in England and Wales.

For support please visit www.forgottenbooks.com

1 MONTH OF FREE READING

at

www.ForgottenBooks.com

By purchasing this book you are eligible for one month membership to ForgottenBooks.com, giving you unlimited access to our entire collection of over 1,000,000 titles via our web site and mobile apps.

To claim your free month visit: www.forgottenbooks.com/free493846

* Offer is valid for 45 days from date of purchase. Terms and conditions apply.

English
Français
Deutsche
Italiano
Español
Português

www.forgottenbooks.com

Mythology Photography **Fiction**
Fishing Christianity **Art** Cooking
Essays Buddhism Freemasonry
Medicine **Biology** Music **Ancient Egypt** Evolution Carpentry Physics
Dance Geology **Mathematics** Fitness
Shakespeare **Folklore** Yoga Marketing
Confidence Immortality Biographies
Poetry **Psychology** Witchcraft
Electronics Chemistry History **Law**
Accounting **Philosophy** Anthropology
Alchemy Drama Quantum Mechanics
Atheism Sexual Health **Ancient History**
Entrepreneurship Languages Sport
Paleontology Needlework Islam
Metaphysics Investment Archaeology
Parenting Statistics Criminology
Motivational

THE BEACON BIOGRAPHIES

EDITED BY

M. A. DeWOLFE HOWE

BENJAMIN FRANKLIN

BY

LINDSAY SWIFT

Copyright 1910 by Small, Maynard & Company

The Beacon Biographies of Eminent Americans

Edited by M. A. DeWolfe Howe

The Summit of Beacon Hill, 1808.

PUBLISHED BY
Small, Maynard & Company
BOSTON

THE Beacon Biographies OF Eminent Americans

Edited by M A DeWolfe Howe

The Summit of Beacon Hill, 1808

PUBLISHED BY
Small Maynard & Company
BOSTON

BENJAMIN FRANKLIN

BY

LINDSAY SWIFT

BOSTON
SMALL, MAYNARD & COMPANY
MDCCCCX

*Copyright, 1910
By Small, Maynard & Company*
(*Incorporated*)

Entered at Stationers' Hall

E 302
.6
F8 S97

Press of
Geo. H. Ellis Co., Boston, U.S.A.

The photogravure used as a frontispiece to this volume is from a small bronze medal in possession of the Boston Public Library. The present engraving is by John Andrew & Son, Boston.

TO
SAMUEL ABBOTT GREEN
WHO HAS INSPIRED MANY TO CHERISH THE MEMORY OF BENJAMIN FRANKLIN

PREFACE

This is not a biography of Benjamin Franklin, nor is it a critical survey of his relations to and services for the young nation of which he was — to use the language of his day — a veritable nursing father. It is more than anything else a series of impressions, brought, I trust, into some kind of harmony and sequence, of the career of the most wonderful American. If the truth about a man may be conceived of as prismatic, then each side of such a life as Franklin lived may be considered, as in his case has often been done well and interestingly, with calmness and balance; but let the crystal be looked at as a whole, and the result is astonishing and dazzling. These impressions have been formed during twenty-five years of a never-wearying intimacy with the great man's doings, sayings, and writings, including three readings of practically all his published works. It is my fault, and not Franklin's, if the enthusiasm of so many years fails to be catching among a few of the possible readers of this endeavour.

To my cherished friend and loyal partner in the building of this small book, Edwin Munroe Bacon, I owe a very keen gratitude. If I furnished most of the timber, he certainly did a generous share in raising the structure, when I needed help as competent as his.

The portrait is from a bronze medallion owned by the Public Library of the City of Boston, and not used so often as to make it other than interesting.

LINDSAY SWIFT.

BOSTON, July 11, 1910.

CHRONOLOGY

1706

Born in Boston, January 17 (January 6, O.S.).

1714

Sent to the grammar school.

1715

Went to a school for writing and arithmetic.

1716

Taken from school to assist his father in the latter's business of tallow-chandler and soap-boiler.

1718

Sent to his cousin Samuel's shop to learn the cutler's trade. Later an apprentice in his brother James's printing-house.

1719

Composed and printed "The Lighthouse Tragedy" and a sailor's song on the "Taking of Teach the Pirate."

1721

Employed on his brother's newspaper, the *New-England Courant*, started this year. Began contributing to its columns under the pseudonym of "Silence Dogood."

1722–23

In charge of the *Courant* during his brother's imprisonment for printing matter objectionable to the authorities, and afterward its ostensible publisher.

1723

Ran away from his brother, and got work in Keimer's printing-house in Philadelphia.

1724

Patronised by Governor Keith, of Pennsylvania. Revisited Boston at Sir William's suggestion to solicit his father's assistance in setting up a printing-house. Failed to obtain it, and later arrived in London, where he found he had been deceived by Keith's promises. Obtained employment in Palmer's printing-house.

CHRONOLOGY

1725–26

Went from Palmer's to Watts's printing-house, where he remained during the rest of his stay in London. Became an expert swimmer, and proposed to set up a swimming school in London. Published (1725) *A Dissertation on Liberty and Necessity, Pleasure and Pain.*

1726

Returned to Philadelphia with Mr. Denham, a Quaker merchant, to enter his employ.

1727

Fell ill of pleurisy, and composed his epitaph. Recovered, and returned to Keimer's printing-house. Employed in Burlington, New Jersey, on a job of printing paper money.

1728

Instituted the Junto, club and debating society. Formed a partnership with Hugh Meredith, and set up for himself.

1729

Took up the publication of the *Pennsylvania Gazette*, and became an editor and public printer. Got the work of printing the Pennsylvania paper money.
Published *A Modest Enquiry into the Nature and Necessity of a Paper-Currency*.

1730

Dissolved partnership with Meredith, and continued alone. Added a little stationer's shop to his business.
September 1, married Deborah Read (then Mrs. Rogers).

1731

Founded the Philadelphia Library.

1732

Began the publication of *Poor Richard's Almanac* (for 1733).
His son Francis Folger Franklin born.

1733

Began the study of modern languages in his spare hours.

1735

Published *A Defense of the Rev. Mr. Hemphill's Observations;*

A Letter to a Friend in the Country, Containing the Substance of a Sermon Preach'd at Philadelphia, in the Congregation of The Rev. Mr. Hemphill;

Some Observations on the Proceedings against The Rev. Mr. Hemphill.

1736

Established the Union Fire Company.

Chosen clerk of the General Assembly of Pennsylvania.

His son Francis died of small-pox.

1737

Appointed postmaster of Philadelphia.

1741

Began the publication of a monthly magazine, the first planned and the second issued in the American colonies. After six months it "quietly expired."

1742

Invented the Franklin stove.

1743
Drew up "Proposals for Establishing an Academy."

1744
Established the American Philosophical Society.

His daughter Sarah born.

Published *An Account Of the New Invented Pennsylvanian Fire-Places.*

1746
His attention first drawn to electricity.

Published *Reflections on Courtship and Marriage: In Two Letters to a Friend.*

1747
Stimulated the establishment of a militia by the government, and fostered the organisation of a voluntary association for the general defence of the city and province.

Published *Plain Truth: Or, Serious Considerations On the Present State of the City of Philadelphia and Province of Pennsylvania.*

1748
Took David Hall as a partner.

1749
Founded his proposed Academy, which became the Academy and Charitable School of the Province of Pennsylvania, and ultimately developed into the University of Pennsylvania.

1751
Published, in London, *Experiments and Observations on Electricity made at Philadelphia in America.*

1752
Proved the identity of electricity and lightning by experimenting with a kite.
Made a member of the Royal Society of London.
Invented the lightning rod.
Elected to civic positions, and a member of the General Assembly for Philadelphia.

1753
Member of a commission from the Council and Assembly to confer with the Indians of Carlisle with respect to a treaty.

1753 (continued)

Appointed, jointly with William Hunter, Postmaster-General of America.

Given the degree of Master of Arts by Harvard College and by Yale College.

Received the Sir Godfrey Copley medal from the Royal Society of London.

Published, in London, *Supplemental Experiments and Observations on Electricity*.

1754

Commissioner for Pennsylvania at a congress of commissioners at Albany to confer with the chiefs of the Six Nations. Drew up his Plan for a Union of the Colonies.

Published, in London, *New Experiments and Observations on Electricity made at Philadelphia in America*.

1755

Aided General Braddock by establishing a system of transportation of military stores.

1756

Entered military service, in charge of the north-western frontier.

1757

Sent to London as agent for the province of Pennsylvania.

1759

Received the degree of Doctor of Laws from the University of St. Andrews, Edinburgh.

Freedom of the city conferred upon him by the corporation of Edinburgh.

Much time this year devoted to electrical experiments in England.

Published, in London, *Some Account of the Success of Inoculation for the Small-Pox in England and America.*

Published, in London, *Parable against Persecution.*

1760

taries brought to a successful close.

First separate edition of the *Way to*

1760 (*continued*)

Wealth ("Father Abraham's Speech," from *Poor Richard's Almanac*) published. Published, in London, *The Interest of Great Britain Considered, With Regard to her Colonies.*

1761

In the autumn made a tour of Holland.

1762

Received the degree of Doctor of Civil Laws from the University of Oxford.

1763

Travelled through the northern colonies to inspect their several post-offices.

Appointed one of the commissioners for Pennsylvania to dispose of the public money appropriated for raising and paying forces to act against the Indians.

1764

Defeated of re-election to the Assembly in an exciting voting contest.

Appointed by the Assembly agent of the

CHRONOLOGY

1764 (continued)

House to present their petition to the King for a change of government.

Sailed for England in November.

Published *A Narrative of the late Massacres, in Lancaster County;*

Cool Thoughts on the Present Situation of our Public Affairs;

A Petition to the King, for changing the Proprietary Government of Pennsylvania into a Royal Government;

Remarks on a late Protest Against the Appointment of Mr. Franklin an Agent for this Province.

1765

Presented to Grenville copy of the resolution of the Pennsylvania Assembly against the proposed Stamp Act.

1766

Efforts to obtain the repeal of the Stamp Act. His examination before the House of Commons, followed by repeal.

Reappointed agent by the Pennsylvania Assembly.

1766 (continued)

Published, in London, *The Examination of Dr. Benjamin Franklin*, etc.

Published, in London, *Physical and Meteorological Observations*.

1768

Authorised to act as agent in London for Georgia.

1769

Chosen by the House of Representatives of New Jersey as agent for that province.

1770

Appointed by the General Court agent for Massachusetts.

1771

Visited Ireland, and received by the Irish Parliament at Dublin. Also visited Scotland.

Wrote the first part of his Autobiography.

1772

Transmitted the Hutchinson-Oliver letters to Massachusetts.

1772 (continued)

Published, in London, *Two Letters, addressed to the Right Rev. Prelates, who a second Time rejected the Dissenters' Bill.*

1773

Examination before the Privy Council on the petition of the Massachusetts Assembly for the removal of Governor Hutchinson.

Published, in the *London Advertiser, Rules for Reducing a Great Empire to a Small One.* Later (1793) issued in pamphlet form.

Published, in London, [Lord Despenser's] *Abridgement of the Book of Common Prayer.* Franklin wrote the preface and abridged the Catechism and Psalms.

1774

Dismissed from the office of deputy postmaster-general of North America.

Published, in London, *Of the Stilling of Waves by means of Oil;*

1774 (*continued*)

Experiments and Observations on Electricity made at Philadelphia.... To which are added, Letters and Papers on Philosophical Subjects.

1775

Returned to Philadelphia.

May 6, elected by the Pennsylvania Assembly a delegate to the Continental Congress. The same month elected Postmaster-General of the colonies.

1776

One of three commissioners sent on a fruitless mission to Canada. Presided over the Constitutional Convention of Pennsylvania. Elected by the Continental Congress one of a committee to frame a Declaration of Independence. Elected one of three commissioners to France. In December arrived in France.

1778

Formally received at the French court. Appointed minister plenipotentiary to France.

1778 (continued)

Issued at Passy the bagatelle, *The Ephemera; an emblem of Human Life.*

1779

Wrote the *Morals of Chess,* afterward published in many editions.
Issued from his press, at Passy, *The Whistle. To Madame Brillon.*

1780

Issued from his press, at Passy, *The Dialogue between Franklin and the Gout.*

1781

Appointed a member of the commission to negotiate a treaty of peace between England and the United States.

1784

Resumed work on his Autobiography.
Issued from his press, at Passy, *Advice to such as would remove to America;* and *Remarks Concerning the Savages of North America.*

1785

His resignation as minister to France accepted by Congress. Returned to Philadelphia in September.

Elected president of the Commonwealth of Pennsylvania.

1786

Re-elected president of Pennsylvania.

Published *Maritime Observations: In a letter from Doctor Franklin to Mr. Alphonsus Le Roy, member of several Academies, in Paris.*

1787

Again re-elected to the presidency of Pennsylvania. Appointed a delegate to the convention which framed the Constitution of the United States.

Published *Observations on the Causes and Cure of Smoky Chimneys.*

1788

Brought the Autobiography down to 1757.

1789

Contributed to the press papers in behalf of the abolition of slavery.

Wrote, but did not publish during his life, *Observations Relative to the Intentions of the Original Founders of the Academy in Philadelphia.*

1790

Died in Philadelphia, April 17, aged eighty-four years and three months.

BENJAMIN FRANKLIN

BENJAMIN FRANKLIN

I.

To send any one who reads these compact pages back to the fount and origin of all essential knowledge of Franklin, his own immortal Autobiography, is motive enough for writing them. Many have considered him, and from various standpoints. In later years Mr. Paul Leicester Ford views him polygonally, Professor McMaster as a man of letters, and Mr. Morse as an American statesman, but all have drawn on the original vintage, reduced to suit a large variety of palates. Parton's second pressing is still so excellent reading that only a condensation of the most straightforward sort can hope to find an excuse for itself on the plea of novelty.

A man who first begins to write of himself when sixty-five years of age is able to discard irrelevancies and to ignore trivialities. With a past of already great achievement and a still more wonderful old age before him, Franklin felt no need for false shame, for it was his object to account for his career and not to extenuate his weaknesses or to magnify his renown. It was with no awkwardness therefore that he speaks of the "poverty and obscurity" in which he was born on January 6 (O.S.), 1706, in the town of Boston, in the Province of Massachusetts-Bay, of Josiah and a second wife Abiah (Folger) Franklin. He was his father's fifteenth child — there being in all seventeen — and his mother's eighth. About where the building formerly occupied by the Boston *Post* now stands, below the corner of Milk Street and Washington, then Marlborough Street, was his birthplace; and on his natal day he was hurried to the Old South Meeting-house opposite — the first South meeting-house that the Old South replaced — and piously dedicated to the God of his fathers, — borne there, so legend has it, in the arms of his own mother. The family, which took its name from the estate of its members as English freeholders, was from Northamptonshire, and, if socially obscure, was not mean. Josiah came with his first wife to New England in 1682: his second wife, Franklin's mother, was the daughter of Peter Folger, "a godly, learned Englishman"; and thus on both sides Franklin came of an unmixed stock, of the sort which takes most kindly and readily to transplantation. He himself was almost a perfect prototype of what we understand to be Americanism,— resourceful, shrewd, somewhat idealistic, and largely practical; as a citizen, generous and helpful; but, as an individual, dextrous to win advantage beyond the point where the scrupulous draw the line.

Franklin went to grammar school when he was eight years old, but "I do not remember when I could not read," he says. From Grandfather Folger he inherited a doleful tendency to verse-making. From his paternal uncle Benjamin, who was also poetically inclined, and who was "a great attender of sermons," he learned a rough sort of shorthand, and received a bent toward books. In arithmetic he "made no progress," though proving himself so fair a scholar in other respects that he was, at ten years of age, put to his father's trade of "sope"-boiling and tallow-chandlering. His astonishing normality was shown by an early desire to go to sea, but he went no further than to sail small boats with other boys. In these sports he was "commonly allowed to govern." The elder Franklin had this aptitude for leadership, and was frequently consulted, by grander people than he himself pretended to be, for his opinion on town and church affairs. Life with the Franklins was simplicity itself. Conversation, meant to be instructive and perhaps elevating, was cultivated. What went into the heads above the board was held to be of more consequence than the food itself. In later years Franklin wrote significantly: "To this day if I am asked I can scarcely tell a few hours after dinner what I dined upon." This indifference to the joys of the palate has been noticed in men of extraordinary ability. Cautious habits and evenness of temperament carried the father through eighty-nine years and the mother through eighty-five years of a life which they undoubtedly enjoyed after their own sober and discreet fashion.

II.

The father's trade was not to the boy's liking, not so much because he felt above it as because it presented to his active mind no healthy and stimulating obstacles. He was already showing aptitude for mechanical devices, and was storing his receptive mind with such reading as he was able to procure with his small spending money. Toward the *Pilgrim's Progress*, Plutarch's *Lives*, and mostly, perhaps, to Cotton Mather's *Essays to do Good*, he shows a deep gratitude. At twelve he was indentured as a printer's apprentice to his brother James till his coming of age, partly because he was bookish and partly because the sea still held out its alluring charms to the restless boy.

His reading, which continued late into the nights, tended to make him disputatious, a fault into which, Franklin says, persons of good sense seldom fall, "except lawyers, university men, and men of all sorts that have been bred at Edinburgh,"— a very sour observation for so complacent a man as Franklin to make, though it betrays the not uncommon suspiciousness of the unacademic mind. Among the various polemics which he held with his chum, John Collins, was one on "the propriety of educating the female sex," in which the young apprentice took, as he usually did, the right side. These and other ambitious strivings to further his knowledge of books and to model himself after the best style, in particular that of the *Spectator*, brought upon him the attention of his own family, if of no one else. His radicalism in matters of religion early showed itself by an evasion, as far as he was able, of "the common attendance on public worship." The eyes of his understanding were levelled in all directions of human interest, usually with entire sanity, sometimes with the perversity of mere youth. He even ventured a prolonged experiment in the vegetable diet, when he was sixteen, and found it intellectually profitable. At this time he happened on three books of particular value to him, Locke's *On the Human Understanding*, *The* [Port Royal] *Art of Thinking*, and the before-mentioned *Essays to do Good*, by Cotton Mather. It is wonderful how readily he seized on the essence of books. His reading in Xenophon's *Memorabilia* helped to lead him into that extremely tolerant method of argument which never forsook him. The Greek restraint and euphemism corresponded happily with his own mental cheerfulness, and he conducted all argumentation with an easy and broad-shouldered effect of strength and responsibility.

Law and journalism have been the two surest roads for American ambition to travel. Benjamin Franklin veered naturally enough into work on his brother James's newspaper, the fourth to be undertaken in the English colonies. There was no legal career open in Boston in those days, but, had there been, the lad would not have been inclined to follow it. The apprentice soon began to send modest contributions to this *New-England Courant*, first anonymously, then openly, somewhat to the irritation of the brother, a rather dour body, who occasionally beat the young contributor, not because the latter was vicious, but because he was abler than his surly master. This fraternal treatment filled Franklin with "that aversion to arbitrary power," as he says, "that has stuck to me through my whole life." A little man would have grown up to bully others as he was himself bullied, but Franklin was small in nothing except his economies, and then only to himself. When James Franklin was imprisoned for publishing matter offensive to the General Court, the younger brother conducted the paper, which a little later by a pardonable trick (in the return of his indenture with his discharge written on the back of it, and the substitution privately of a new one for the remainder of the term) appeared under the name of Benjamin Franklin. One trick led to another. The new publisher, having secured his indenture, soon refused to hold himself bound by the new and secret agreement, and left his brother. For this he was promptly blacklisted by all the master printers in Boston, and this experience sent him at the age of seventeen on a three days' voyage, in company with his friend Collins, to New York, and thence, finding no employment there, on a turbulent passage to New Jersey, and overland, mostly on foot, to Philadelphia.

III.

EARLY on a Sunday morning, clad in workaday clothes and travel-stained, Benjamin Franklin arrived in this enterprising town, which henceforth was to divide the honours with Boston as having fostered the most comprehensive genius of American life. With a Dutch dollar and a shilling's worth of copper in his pocket the Boston-bred lad sought to buy "bisket," but had to content himself with three penny rolls. After sauntering past the house where lived Deborah Read, who was later to be his wife, he found himself in a Quaker meeting-house, where he fell asleep.

He soon secured employment with one Keimer, a rather inefficient printer, the poorer of the only two then in Philadelphia, who, himself an author, was fonder of books than of making them. Lodging was taken with Mr. Read, and Franklin began to live comfortably, "forgetting Boston as much as he could." Being of good address, he won the attention of Sir William Keith, governor of the province, who would have the boy to dine occasionally at his own table, much to the astonishment of Keimer. Encouraged by offers of the governor to turn the public printing into his hands if he would set up on his own account, and by the promise of Sir William that, to obtain Josiah Franklin's assistance in the venture, he would undertake to reconcile the father and son, Franklin took passage for Boston in April, 1724, after seven months' absence.

Though this unbiblical prodigal returned, to the joy of his family, with five pounds sterling in his pocket, the elder brother carried out his part of the familiar parable by turning his back on such audacious prosperity. James Franklin was something of a churl, and this visit, in which were flourished dazzling handfuls of silver, "offended him extremely." Josiah Franklin declined, though courteously, Governor Keith's suggestion that he set up the enterprising young printer in business, but was evidently impressed by the attention of so important a personage. The frugal old man gave his approbation and blessing to his son as he started for New York by the way of Newport, where lived Benjamin's brother John, who was glad to see his relative, and commissioned him to collect a considerable debt. The voyage from Newport to New York was safely passed. There his old chum Collins again crossed his adventurous way, changed by brandy-drinking from an industrious and studious lad into a purposeless young man. The sturdy printer, not deserting his besotted friend, took him in tow to Philadelphia. Not long afterward Collins, still in debt to his benefactor, took passage for the Barbadoes, and disappeared from Franklin's ken. At this time was committed one of those "errata" of which Franklin, in a sort of lustratory mood, was fond of confessing. This erratum was, in plain, the embezzlement of money which he had been charged to collect for a trustful New Englander, a friend of his brother John. The sin was committed, as this sin so often is, not to help himself, but another,—the worthless Collins.

It was also about this time that, tempted by that most irresistible of all odours to the hungry man,— fried fish,— he abjured vegetarianism and fell back for a while amiably into the dietary traces. But he continued to experiment with food, and induced the long-bearded and gluttonous Keimer, with whom he had again resumed business relations, to adopt a simple method, at a cost of eighteen pence a week each, until Keimer weakly fell from grace under the blandishments of roast pig. Self-improvement in one way and another was never out of Franklin's mind, and his determination and fixity of purpose are never better shown than by his friendships, especially with men of his own age. Osborne, Watson, and Ralph, who afterward became a literary man in a small way, and Benjamin himself took Sunday strolls, argued, compared notes, criticised each other freely, though in the main amiably.

In his nineteenth year, having come to a good understanding with Miss Read as to the strength of their mutual affection, and having taken berth with Ralph on the "annual ship" which plied between London and Philadelphia, Franklin, within a few days of his nineteenth birthday, reached London on December 24, 1724.

IV.

FRANKLIN at once learned that he had been lied to by Governor Sir William Keith, by whose flatteries and promises he had been led to take this voyage. Humbugged as he was by the great man, imperturbable good nature led him to write Keith down as "otherwise an ingenious, sensible man, a pretty good writer, and good governor for the people."

Ralph became a hanger-on at the literary and theatrical kennels of the day, while his virtuous pal went to his trade at Palmer's shop in Bartholomew Close. A very good specimen of Franklin's skill in composition at this time exists in the second edition of Wollaston's *Religion of Nature,* to which Franklin wrote a reply, *A Dissertation on Liberty and Necessity, Pleasure and Pain,* which proved too sceptical to suit his master. This pamphlet was "another erratum," not so great a one, however, as forgetting "by degrees" the engagement with Miss Read, and omitting to write her more than one letter, and that one only to tell her that he was "not likely soon to return."

The next erratum was more serious, but frankly told. Ralph, forgetting his own wife and child, had taken up with a young milliner. In Ralph's absence from London his friend sought to take his place. The lady's affections, if irregular, were loyal, and Franklin was not only discomfited, but by his treachery gave the poetaster a chance to relieve his jealous anger by repudiating all former obligations, monetary and other, to his more prudent associate.

Franklin's literary venture with the *Religion of Nature* brought him into some vivacious company of a bookish turn who gathered at an ale-house. From that time on till his first experience in London ended he worked at Watts's printing-house, near Lincoln's Inn Fields. It was here that he set his intemperate fellows the admirable example of not drinking beer during working hours. He kept himself strong and well on water, while they guzzled after the immutable fashion of the British workman. "Thus," he rather sadly comments, "these poor devils keep themselves always under." Failing, on a change of work, to set up the usual five shillings for drink, Benjamin was so thoroughly ignored, and so worried by the "chappel ghost," that he at last yielded to his tormentors. He was, however, able to bring the force of his example to bear on some of the printers in regard to habits of food and drink, and the shrine of St. Monday was correspondingly deserted.

The young American's bodily strength was then as remarkable as his mental vigour. He could carry upstairs and down a large locked "form" of type in each hand,—a feat at which his fellows wondered, for one form at a time was usually carried, requiring the use of both arms. At swimming he was from boyhood to mature life a marvel. On one occasion he swam from Chelsea to Blackfriars, "performing on the way many feats of activity." Years afterward he suggested that the Channel might be crossed by a swimmer lying on his back and drawn by a kite. Fearless in all experimentation, it is a wonder that Franklin did not essay this feat himself. So fond, indeed, was he of fresh air and clean water that he seems almost to have discovered their hygienic uses to men. In this as in many other ways he was essentially a modern.

Tired at last of London, he agreed with Mr. Denham, an old Quaker merchant then there, to return to Philadelphia as his clerk for fifty pounds a year, Pennsylvania money,—a less sum than he was earning in England. It is fortunate that he so planned, else had he been tempted, under the patronage of Sir William Wyndham, to open a swimming school.

After eighteen months spent sometimes in folly, but mostly in wise living, Franklin sailed on July 23, 1726, from Gravesend, a "cursed biting place." "Albion, farewell!" he exclaims in his lively journal of the voyage, as he watches the cliffs of England fade. The weariness of travel was relieved at draughts, a game in which he much delighted, and then again at cards. Franklin sagely observes that one should not care for consequences in play, for, of two persons equal in skill, he who has the more anxiety is sure to lose. What with philosophical and social observations, the catching of dolphins, the meeting and passing of vessels, the voyage wore on, till at the end of about ten weeks the young Franklin began to feel the exhilaration common to all who have sailed westward from the fogs and clouds of England to the gay, clear air of America, and presently he was again at home in Philadelphia.

V.

ON landing, he soon learned that his neglect of Miss Read had borne fruit, for she had been induced by friends to marry a worthless potter, named Rogers, who soon ran off to the West Indies, where he supposedly died.

Franklin's new employer, Denham, opened a store, and gave him a large responsibility in the venture, until both fell sick. Franklin was brought so low by pleurisy that he felt loath to recover. Economical even when bargaining with death, he felt that, if he lived, he should "have all that disagreeable work to do over again." A virtuous contempt of the incident of dissolution was characteristic of his large nature, though he was prudent to a degree in matters of health and wise living.

On the death of Denham and after some hesitation, Franklin again entered Keimer's employ, and brought the latter's printing business up to a better standard. His resourcefulness led him to make moulds and matrices to supply a sad deficiency of "sorts," to engrave occasionally, and to make ink. So useful a servant, if he works unselfishly, is seldom appreciated, and it was in the order of human nature that the fatuous Keimer should find an early occasion to dismiss his factotum. For a short time he returned to Keimer's office to help him out on a job of printing paper money for New Jersey, to facilitate which Franklin contrived a copper-plate press. Meanwhile he had arranged with a Welshman, Hugh Meredith, also an employé of Keimer's, whom Franklin had helped to forsake strong drink, to set up a separate establishment.

The Autobiography halts at this place a moment to explain its author's attitude at that time toward religion and morals. Brought up by his parents "piously in the Dissenting way," he found himself at fifteen no little of a sceptic. Perversely turned in favour of Deism by reading some of Sir Robert Boyle's Lectures which were directed against it, he came to regard the optimistic conclusions of the deistic doctrine of little practical value. While still rejecting Revelation, he did, however, hold fast to the certitudes that "truth, sincerity and integrity" were of prime importance. He thus was able to assert that he had a "tolerable character to begin the world with," though in his original draught he states that there were some foolish intrigues with low women,— an admission which he allowed himself on the margin to modify considerably. No trace of spiritual exaltation appears in this frank confession, but there is at all times evident a reaching forward to a homely, practical, and not unworthy standard of life.

The year of his start with Meredith, or in 1728, he had founded the Junto, first called the Leather Apron, that small but admirable beginning of greater things. On Friday evenings this little club met to discuss philosophy, morals, and doubtless the questions of the day, in a spirit of equanimity and good faith. The first members were a scrivener's clerk, a mathematician, a surveyor, a shoemaker, afterward a mathematician, a joiner, a merchant's clerk, Franklin himself, and three fellow-workmen of his at Keimer's. Two of these associates afterward became surveyors-general, and one a merchant of note; but the names of all of them have passed into oblivion, except that of the founder. Many and varied were the questions put and answered, and great was the indirect good done these young men by their serious endeavour.

It was a time of prodigious industry for the young firm, and twenty-four hours were hardly long enough to suit their measure of the day. "The industry of that Franklin," said Dr. Baird, a Scotchman, "is superior to anything I ever saw of the kind; I see him still at work when I go home from the club; and he is at work again before his neighbours are out of bed."

By a little manœuvring Franklin at the age of twenty-three (1729) came into possession of a paper which Keimer, secretly informed of a similar intention on Franklin's part, had started, but which languished for about nine months on a subscription list of not more than ninety names. This paper was speedily turned into the famous *Pennsylvania Gazette*, and soon gave its publisher not only reputation, but good returns, though Keimer in his announcement admitted that it did not so "quadrate" with his circumstances as to enable him to go on with the venture. Meredith, Franklin's partner, had the failing common to printers in those days, and was no help. The inability of Meredith's father to come forward with a promised loan would have thrown the already prosperous *Gazette* into difficulties, had it not been for the loyal offer of two Junto friends, Coleman and Grace. Easy terms were made with Meredith to withdraw, and the partnership was dissolved in July, 1730.

The previous year Franklin wrote and published *A Modest Enquiry into the Nature and Necessity of a Paper-Currency*, which was a powerful stimulant to the cause of paper money, then popular, though "the rich men disliked it." More currency was issued, and Franklin was given the job of printing it,—"a very profitable jobb," as he says, and not put down as one of his errata. In ten years the volume of paper had increased from £15,000 to £80,000, and gave much temporary prosperity, though Franklin later admitted that "there are limits beyond which the quantity may be hurtful."

Business was now rushing with the young printer-editor. He added a stationer's shop, and began to pay his debts. He studied frugality as a science, and gave attention to personal appearance. Ostentatiously, he would sometimes wheel his paper stock home on a barrow *à la* honest tradesman, for even a great man may be a prig. Franklin never went "a fishing or shooting," and only read books because the doing so was "seldom, snug and gave no scandal." No wonder he grew prosperous! Meanwhile Keimer and his luckless successor, Harry, failed and went to the Barbadoes, leaving Bradford as Franklin's sole competitor in Philadelphia.

The wife of Godfrey, the glazier, at whose house Franklin was then living, thought the rising young man would make a fit mate for the daughter of a relation. Franklin was not coy or ill-disposed to the match, but, the settlement being less than would suffice to pay his printing-house debts, he calmly suggested that the parents of the girl mortgage their house to make up the sum! This affair fell through, but left him favourably inclined to the wedded state. Intimacy began again with the Read family, and he was married to Deborah on September 1, 1730. Franklin, if shrewd, was venturesome, and this marriage, postponed by his own none too scrupulous neglect, was in keeping with his willingness to run a fair risk for a good bargain. There was no certainty in regard to the supposed death of Miss Read's first husband, and this may have been thought by Franklin to be an offset to the wretched irregularities in which he admits that he had been engaged just before his taking a wife. Such follies were the commonplace wanderings of unrestrained youth, and his discerning mind, if not the loftiness of his ideals, soon taught him the essential vulgarity of promiscuous unchastity. Balancing then the possible illegality of the marriage against his own rather timorous wantonness, the couple took their chances, and the venture prospered.

With this important event ends that part of the Autobiography begun in 1771, while Franklin, then agent of the colonies, was staying in England with his friend, Bishop Shipley. Not until he was at Passy, in 1784, as minister to France, did he again take up the narrative.

VI.

He was particularly urged to this second effort to complete his masterpiece by his friend Benjamin Vaughan, who wanted to see Franklin's career placed in comparison "with the lives of various public cut-throats and intriguers, and with absurd monastic self-tormentors or vain literary triflers." The sincere wishes of a friend prevailed on the old man's feelings, and he begins again by rehearsing with commendable pride his share in starting what proved to be in effect, if not in name, the first public library in this country.

Books and bookshops in 1730 were few in the towns of Philadelphia and New York. There was intellectual life in Boston, then the chief town of the colonies, but certainly no irradiating literary influence. The base of mental supplies was London, and London was a long way off. About fifty subscribers of forty shillings each down, and ten shillings a year thereafter, were found willing to start the scheme of a subscription library. In this project, as in everything else, Franklin showed his incomparable good sense by putting himself behind the vague shelter of a "number of friends," who had urged him to start the scheme. Most of the subscribers were young tradesmen, naturally jealous of any one who showed himself forthputting. Thus early Franklin learned that the hidden is the stronger power, and that only small men "claim" merit for deeds performed.

He began, he tells us, to thrive wonderfully in his business and in his general life. His wife was no laggard herself, and helped her husband in ways not commonly thought possible or desirable by less clever women. Yet it was thrifty Deborah who first introduced luxury into the household in the shape of a china bowl and a silver spoon.

This extravagance was, as a matter of course, intended for her honoured husband, who years later, when in London, used to send her all manner of fine things, rich patterns of cloths, and the latest thing from the London shops. The Franklins grew to love comfortable and ample living, but never with ostentation. He found it possible to live many years away from his "dear child," as he always called her in his letters, but he never forgot her or the fact that she was a woman with tastes and fancies. This loyalty to each other was of a varying character, but the existence of it cannot be doubted. He pays full tribute to her worth in the Autobiography.

Concrete expression of American humour definitely began in the year 1732, when the first issue of *Poor Richard's Almanac* appeared. There was already the spoken word of Yankee wit, Dutch phlegm, Pennsylvania shrewdness, and all the incipient and various particles of what even as early as the Revolution had begun to shape into a national way of looking at the minor tragedies and comedies of domestic and civil life in that quizzical, consciously shy, and self-deprecating way that the world calls American. In the cool, dry ichor of Franklin's veins ran all the potentialities of this God-given racial quality. For twenty-five years this *Almanac*, successful from the start, gave forth annually and abundantly the fertile humour of Richard Saunders. Homely wisdom, good sense, jests, both broad and keen as the license of the times allowed, continued long to amuse and instruct the English Colonies of North America. In 1757 Franklin garnered the best of these proverbs and *mots* into a sort of logical continuity, first known as *Father Abraham's Speech*, but passed into universal knowledge under the name of *The Way to Wealth*. It may safely be said that it is the American classic *par excellence*, and shares with

Mrs. Stowe's *Uncle Tom's Cabin* the honour of having passed by translation into more other tongues than anything else thus far bearing the stamp of our national spirit.

He was meanwhile making a success of his paper, introducing modern ideas into its columns and lifting journalism above the personalities and narrowness of a provincial press. He was as good a newspaper man in his day as Greeley in his. It is hard to think of Franklin as having at that time moments of leisure, yet he continued to wander a little afield by espousing the cause of a young Irish Presbyterian preacher named Hemphill, and even wrote a few controversial sermons for his friend. He also gave his scant spare hours to the study of languages, beginning with French, of which he soon made himself so much a master "as to be able to read the books with ease." Then he undertook Italian, pursuing this study along with chess, playing under an agreement with his fellow-player, another student, that the victor in every game should impose a task in grammar or translation which the vanquished must perform upon honour before the next meeting. "As we played pretty equally we thus beat one another into that language."

He lost in the year 1736, of small-pox, Francis Folger Franklin, his only son born in wedlock. It was Franklin's regret that the child had not been inoculated, for it was not his way to neglect any method which pointed forward. His only other child born in lawful wedlock was his daughter Sarah, usually called Sally, born September 11, 1744. She married in 1767 Richard Bache, of Philadelphia, and from her have descended all in whose veins runs legitimately the Benjamin Franklin blood. The same year that his little Frank died he was chosen to the lucrative position of clerk of the General Assembly. About this time he found opportunity to visit

Boston, from which he had been absent for ten years. Returning thence, he went to Newport, where now lived his brother James, though in declining health.

The now prospering young printer usually kept good company, and, if he could not always enjoy the society of superiors, took rather good care that his equals were of the right sort. But in the year 1737 he seems to have fallen into evil hands, and the short experience did him no good. He was a Freemason, and respected his relation with the Masonic body to the day of his death. He permitted himself, however, to take part, a very small part, in the mock initiation of a young apprentice who wished to join the order. The youth's master and others indulged in various forms of horse-play which eventually led to the would-be novitiate's death. Franklin was not present at the tragic ceremonies, and in fact had even withdrawn himself from participation in the indecencies practised on the witless youth. The whole affair was not in consonance with the general character of Franklin, who never showed, so far as his own words disclose, any fondness for practical jokes or other boisterous conduct. It was an erratum which he passes by in his Autobiography unnoticed, but Bradford in the *Mercury* made the most of the incident.

The same year of this untoward happening, however, Franklin received the postmastership of which Bradford had been relieved for inefficiency, and particularly for failures to make any returns whatever of his accounts to the general office for over five years. This position naturally tended to increase his already swelling good fortune, and he was able, by reason of the opportunity which success affords, to give himself more largely to the public welfare. His newspaper, thanks to the wider channel made for its circulation through the post-office, spread in influence and paid well,—so well, in fact, that the editor fell into a temptation common to men of push and enterprise. He wanted to start a magazine, and felt so pleased with the idea that, in spite of his wise adage about keeping secrets to one's self, he whispered the scheme. Another publisher was infected with the idea, and Franklin's *The General Magazine*, which appeared on February 16, 1741, was antedated by *The American Magazine* by just three days. Had Franklin held his tongue,—as he so often advised others to do,—he would have had the honour of publishing the first American specimen of periodical literature. His rival, Andrew Bradford, gave up after issuing three numbers, but Franklin held out for six months, and then, after considerable loss, stopped his magazine, which was very creditable in appearance, though totally unlike the rest of Franklin's usual typographical work.

Curiously, there was a later *American Magazine* published in Boston from 1743 to 1746, in the imprint of which Franklin appears as the seller in Philadelphia. It was a more imposing affair, and marked a step in advance of Franklin's modest venture, which, however, had a quiet distinction of its own with its "Ich dien" plumes on the neat title-page and a generally trig look withal. If it was his first essay into side paths of publishing, it was also the last, and we must remember that he had not the whitened bones of other adventurers to deter him from this erratum,—one of which he says nothing in his Autobiography. One peculiarity of this short-lived magazine was that it had and sought no subscriptions, but tried to depend on the merit of each issue for the favour of the public.

With about fifteen brother printers, mostly young men, "staked" by him in five colonies as well as in Jamaica and

Antigua, from whom he drew, as a rule, a third of the profits made by each; with a prosperous newspaper and a popular and also lucrative almanac; with the printing of the colony's paper money safe in his own hands, as well as the power which the postmastership necessarily conferred upon him,— it is no wonder that Benjamin Franklin waxed powerful, and that Mr. Smyth, his latest biographer, found in his career at this time a forecast of the merger, or trust, of to-day. He did not, however, grow ostentatious in proportion to his growing wealth and power, but tried faithfully to live up to the thrifty inculcations of his own Poor Richard.

By 1748, when only forty-two years old, he began to dream, like a European, of preparing for old age and its well-established comforts. David Hall, a Scotchman, recommended to him by William Strahan, his English printer-friend, had for several years been his active and capable partner. Having put his printing-house under the care of this partner and having absolutely left off bookselling and removed to a quieter part of the town, Franklin now hoped to be quite master of his own time,—"no longer, as the song has it, at every one's call but my own." Cherishing the same hope, he had refused engaging further in public affairs. "Thus you see," he wrote his friend Colden, "I am in a fair way of having no other tasks but such as I shall like to give myself, and of enjoying what I look upon as a great happiness, leisure to read, study, make experiments, and converse at large with such ingenious and worthy men as are pleased to honour me with their friendship or acquaintance, on such points as may produce something for the common benefit of mankind, uninterrupted by the little cares and fatigues of business." Could there have been a greater delusion than this pretty programme?

VII.

FRANKLIN does not label all his wanderings "errata," but is so frank about stating them that it may well be doubted whether he knew his moral bearings at times. When he was chosen clerk of the General Assembly of Pennsylvania (1736), he soon saw that the position was not only a good one in itself, but that it enabled him to "work" the members to get legislative printing into his own hands. This and "other occasional jobbs" were clear instances of "graft" in its primitive sense, where a man secures an extraordinary advantage or profit, aside from his salary, by reason of holding a certain office. But these were the days of the Walpole administration in the mother-country, and a young printer, with his fortune still to make, had no loud call to be sensitive in such matters when English statesmen were setting the worst possible example. It is wholly probable that to the insensitive Franklin "jobbs" of this sort were the properest way in the world of getting ahead. The next year he stepped into the deputy postmaster-generalship in Philadelphia only to find that his newspaper grew apace when his own hands ran the machinery by which he could distribute it more readily and receive more advertisements and correspondence from a wider field. Instead of revenging himself on Bradford who had found ways, when he was in office, to hinder the course of Franklin's paper through the mails, he adopted no cheap methods to injure his old rival.

The associations of young men in this country for self-betterment have, since early colonial days, in many cases, perhaps in most cases, frequently found themselves drifting into the absorbing life of local politics. They were potent just before the Revolution, and even in anti-slavery days found ready opportunity to depart from their original purposes. Some of them had an influence which in these more critical times would be considered baneful. In a cruder period their reaching out into a wider field was normal and, in the main, desirable. The Junto, for which Franklin kept his affection as long as he lived, was no exception to the general trend of such organisations. As a rising man and an influential member of this club, and also as an office-holder, the editor-printer turned his attention to what we should now call civic betterment. The tip-staff in all ages has been something of a *mauvais sujet*, and so Franklin, seeing the demoralised condition of the city watch, unfolded his plans for one more means of raising taxes to support a constabulary. Soon this reform went through. Next he brought about an interest in better protection against fire, and writing in 1784, when he was an old man, he had the satisfaction of saying that he and one other still survived the other original members of the Union Fire Company, set on its feet in 1736, by the agency of which Philadelphia was so well equipped that he doubted whether there was "a city in the world better provided with the means of putting a stop to beginning conflagrations." In both these excellent reforms the Junto took the leading part, but Franklin was the master spirit. Another wholesome project started by him was the proper cleaning of streets, not only in Philadelphia, but later in London. He certainly was profiting by the exhortations of his boyish Dogood Papers in his brother's *New-England Courant*.

At the same time with his efforts toward civic betterment he was advancing reforms in the province. While, as he wrote in the Autobiography, he had "on the whole abundant reason to be satisfied with" his "being established in Pennsylvania," there were two things he regretted, "there being no provision for defence nor for a compleat education of youth: no militia, no college." To meet the latter defect, he drew up his "Proposal for Establishing an Academy," in 1743, from which ultimately came the "Academy and Charitable School of the Province of Pennsylvania," the nucleus of the noble University of Pennsylvania. The former deficiency was overcome through his publication in 1747 of his pamphlet *Plain Truth*, written to promote a voluntary association of the people for the defence of the province against possible encroachments of the Spanish and the French, the long-continued endeavours of the governor to prevail with the Quaker Assembly to pass a militia law and make other provisions for defence having proved abortive. Through his spirited leadership the voluntary association organised into companies and regiments, and he supplied devices and mottoes which were painted on silk flags provided the companies by the patriotic women of Philadelphia. The building of a battery below the town, with means furnished by a lottery, was also stimulated by him.

Meanwhile he was serenely pursuing his experiments and philosophical studies. He had already invented the Franklin stove, the Pennsylvania fireplace, as he termed it, and declined a patent for it upon the high principle "that as we enjoy great advantages from the inventions of others we should be glad of an opportunity to serve others by any invention of ours; and this we should do freely and generously." The next year, 1744, he laid the foundations for the American Philosophical Society "for promoting useful knowledge among the British Plantations of America," and for corresponding with the learned societies of Europe; and in 1746 he had begun his electrical experiments, in which his advance was so rapid that in a very few years he had proved the "sameness" of lightning with electricity, had made his famous demonstration with the kite, had invented the lightning rod, and had been elected to the Royal Society upon his merits as a scientist.

By 1752 he was again in active public service, busied in many affairs. He was made an alderman of the city, and was elected to the General Assembly. He tried a little the office of justice of the peace by attending a few courts and sitting on the bench to hear causes; but, finding that he did not possess a sufficient knowledge of the common law "to act in that station with credit," he wisely withdrew from it. Upon taking his seat in the General Assembly, election to which was repeated annually for ten years, "without my ever asking any elector for his vote, or signifying directly or indirectly any desire of being chosen," he so worked his influence as to turn over the lucrative clerkship to his son William, born out of wedlock and taken magnanimously into the new household by Mrs. Franklin on her marriage. The next year he was appointed one of the commissioners to confer with the Indians of Carlisle, the result of which was a satisfactory treaty, and in course of time his pamphlet, *Remarks Concerning the Savages of North America*. The same year came his appointment, jointly with William Hunter, as Postmaster-General of America by a commission from the Postmaster-General in England. The business of the office then occasioned his taking a journey to New England, and while he was there Harvard gave him the degree of Master of Arts, with which Yale had already honoured him, in consideration of his electrical discoveries. The following year (1754), when war with France was again threatening, he went to Albany as a representative from Pennsylvania to the congress of commissioners from the several colonies to confer with the chiefs of the Six Nations concerning means for mutual defence. On this occasion he projected and drew his famous plan for the union of the colonies under one government, known as the "Plan of Union," which failed of adoption, the colonial assemblies objecting because "there was too much prerogative in it," while "in England it was judg'd to have too much of the democratic."

The next year he is found aiding General Braddock at Fredericktown, in stress for facilities to transport his stores and military baggage, by the establishment of a system of teams and packhorses, with such success and promptitude that in less than two weeks "one hundred and fifty waggons with two hundred and fifty-nine carrying horses were on their march for the camp," while Braddock's men, after scouring the country roundabout, had been unable to collect more than twenty-five teams, and not all of them in serviceable condition. He further aided this unhappy general materially by arranging for the sending of supplies of provisions after him upon the march, advancing for the service a thousand pounds of his (Franklin's) own money. He rated Braddock as he stands in history: "The general was, I think, a brave man, and might probably have made a figure as a good officer in some European war. But he had too much self-confidence, too high an opinion of the validity of regular troops, and too mean a one of both Americans and Indians."

After Braddock's defeat his own military service began with his acceptance, in December, of the command of the troops to defend the frontier, and his departure with his son William as aide-de-camp.

VIII.

It was the punctiliousness of the Proprietary Government of Pennsylvania, through its representative, Governor Denny (who had brought back with him the gold Sir Godfrey Copley medal presented some time before by the Royal Society to Franklin), which occasioned the first sending of Franklin in an official capacity to England. The first month of 1756 had been spent by him in efficient military service on the frontier, in the last French and Indian war. He raised and disciplined troops, established blockhouses, and erected Fort Allen on the site of the completely destroyed village of Gnadenhütten. Content, apparently, with his share of glory, he had declined Governor Morris's promise to make him a general if he would move on Fort Duquesne, and his military honours rest on his title of Colonel of the Regiment of Philadelphia, which he accepted shortly after. Affairs were in so bad a condition, the losses by death and destruction of property so great, that it was felt imperative to raise funds to protect the province. The budget consented to by the Assembly fell under that estimated by the governor, who threw it out. It was time to present matters before a more effective authority than the protector of the interests of the Penns, and accordingly, in February, 1757, Franklin was appointed agent of the province "to solicit and transact the affairs thereof in Great Britain." The issue was the right of taxing the proprietary estate in common with the estates of the people.

The Proprietaries seem to have been anxious to propitiate Franklin through Denny, who, inspired by too much madeira and a certain natural stupidity, tried to offer "inducements" to the most astute man in Pennsylvania. Franklin always knew on which side his bread was buttered, and he also knew the simple elements of right and wrong. Therefore, he would have none of this blundering effort at bribery, and adhered to the popular side. On the failure of the governor, who seems to have maintained agreeable personal relations with the unruly commoner, the Assembly determined to resist the obstructive policy of the Proprietaries by thus sending Franklin to England.

Then appeared Lord Loudon, who managed to patch up some sort of armistice before Franklin sailed, and then decided to sail on the packet with Franklin, to join the fleet headed for Louisburg. If ever a man deserved the titular distinction of "Cunctator," Loudon is that man. Franklin arrived in New York about the first of April, his "sea-stores" already gone ahead of him, and June had nearly passed before he sailed, owing to Loudon's delays and indecisions. The governor's messenger,

Innis, said of this Fabian worthy that he was "like St. George on the signs, always on horseback and never rides on." Finally, after breaking away from Loudon, who did not go to Louisburg after all, Franklin arrived in London late in July, 1757.

He was sought at once by distinguished men of science and was honoured in various ways, but, true to his early calling, he looked up his printing associates of thirty years before and "set up" the beer, the drinking of which he had sedulously tried to stop or diminish when he was a London printer bent on improving the world after his own standards.

Soon after his arrival a meeting was arranged, through Dr. John Fothergill, with the Proprietaries at the house of Thomas Penn in Spring Garden. They were represented by Mr. Paris as counsel, a "proud, angry man," with whom Franklin soon refused to parley.

Franklin's minutes of complaints were then put into the hands of the attorney and solicitor-general for their opinion. A year went by, and no answer to Franklin was forthcoming. A message was finally sent direct to the Assembly, in no way meeting Franklin's complaints, but stating that some terms could be arrived at if the Assembly "would send out some person of candour." The message was not answered because Denny agreed to an act taxing the proprietary estate. The objection of the Proprietaries naturally followed, but the act was sustained in the main, because Lord Mansfield accepted the assurance of Franklin that no injury would accrue to the proprietary estate in case the act were executed. Thus his first great venture into the field of high negotiations was a success.

There is no pleasanter episode in Franklin's life than his experiences, first begun on this mission, at No. 7

Craven Street, Strand, where he lived in great comfort in the lodgings of Mrs. Margaret Stevenson, with whom and her daughter Mary his friendship lasted for many years.

IX.

ALTHOUGH this first mission was brought to a close in the summer of 1760, Franklin remained in England two years longer. While the slow-moving negotiations were under way, he had employed his ample leisure in further electrical experiments, scientific studies, and philosophical speculations; had enjoyed his association with men of learning; had travelled about England and also into Scotland, where he spent six weeks of the "densest happiness" he had "met with in any part of" his life; had visited the home of his ancestors; had written more essays and skits; had carried on a voluminous correspondence; and had in 1759 received the degree of Doctor of Laws from the University of St. Andrews at Edinburgh, to be followed three years later by the honorary doctorate of civil law from the University of Oxford.

With his mission off his hands, the remaining two years were largely given to his advocacy of the retention of Canada and its annexation to the British empire, an end which was directly influenced by his contributions to the public press and the publication of the vigorous anonymous pamphlet, *The Interest of Great Britain Considered, With Regard to her Colonies, And the Acquisition of Canada and Guadaloupe,* now known to have been written by him with the aid of his associate, Richard Jackson.

In the summer of 1761 he made the tour of the Low Countries, returning to London in season to witness the coronation of George III. in September; and the next summer he sailed for home, after having had "a most agreeable time of it in Europe." He had added to his circle numerous valued friends, had contracted rare new friendships, and had been flattered with much notice by persons of distinction. It was shortly before his departure that David Hume wrote him, "America has sent us many good things, gold, silver, sugar, tobacco, indigo &c.; but you are the first philosopher, and indeed the first great man of letters for whom we are beholden to her." The return voyage, too, contributed to his entertainment. He sailed in late August in company with ten merchant-ships under a convoy of a man-of-war, and the weather was so favourable that "there were few days in which we could not visit from ship to ship, dining with each other and on board the man-of-war: which made the time pass agreeably, much more so than when one goes in a single ship, for this was like travelling in a moving village with all one's neighbours about one."

He reached Philadelphia on the first of November, and arrived "safe and well at my own door." He found his wife and daughter in good health, "the latter grown quite a woman, with many amiable accomplishments" acquired in his absence of nearly six years; and his friends "as hearty and affectionate as ever, with whom my house was filled for many days to congratulate me on my return."

He was soon again immersed in public affairs. Upon his reappearance in the Assembly he was voted three thousand pounds sterling for his services in England and "their thanks delivered by the Speaker." In the following spring, 1763, he set out on a tour of the northern colonies to inspect and regulate their post-offices, and in this journey spent the summer, travelling some sixteen hundred miles. Through the following winter, during which the Assembly sat, "business publick and private," he wrote, "devours all my time." Besides his duty as an assemblyman, he had another trust to execute, that "of being one of the commissioners appointed by law to dispose of the public money appropriated to the raising and paying of an army to act against the Indians and defend the frontiers." Meanwhile arose the two insurrections in December of the "back inhabitants" of the province,—chiefly Scotch-Irish frontiersmen who conceived the idea that the Quaker Assembly would fail to provide adequate defences. Twenty poor Indians, who had from the first settlement of the province lived in peace under the protection of the government, were barbarously massacred. This roused Franklin's indignation and gave him "a good deal of employment," for the rioters threatened further mischief and their actions were seemingly approved by an increasing party. To strengthen the hands of the weak government by rendering the rioters' acts unpopular and odious, he issued his fiery pamphlet, *A Narrative of the late Massacres, in Lancaster County, of a Number of Indians, Friends of this Province, by Persons Unknown.* It had the effect intended, and afterward, when a body of the rioters marched toward the capital in defiance of the government, with the avowed intent of killing one hundred and forty Indian converts under its protection, he found little difficulty in promptly forming, at the governor's request, an association of a thousand men with arms for the defence of the government and the Indians. In this crisis the governor, now John Penn, made Franklin's house for some time his headquarters, and did everything by his advice, "so that for about forty-eight hours I was a very great man." The fighting face that the defenders put on, and the reasonings they used with the insurgents, — Franklin was sent out with three others to "meet and discourse them," — turned them back and restored quiet to the city. Then he "became a less man than ever," for by his pamphlet and these transactions he made himself many enemies among the populace, and, seeing in this an opportunity long desired by the proprietary interests for his overthrow, the governor, despite the services Franklin had just rendered, joined the whole weight of this interest to get him out of the Assembly. At the next election, accordingly, a majority of "about twenty-five in four thousand" managed to defeat the now undesirable candidate. There was a lively time in old Philadelphia on voting day, and things were done according to the most approved modern methods to defeat the illustrious commoner.

X.

CLOSE upon his defeat as candidate for membership to the Assembly came his election by a vote of nineteen to eleven in that body to present to the king the petition, as aid to Richard Jackson, the provincial agent of Pennsylvania, which should perchance hasten a royal instead of a proprietary government. John Dickinson, one of those virtuous men of great ability whose genius leads them unerringly a few points off the true course, fought against this appointment of "the man most obnoxious to his country"; but in spite of this alleged public odium Benjamin Franklin, who replied to these and other aspersions with an exasperating and well-calculated moderation, was accompanied, entirely to his own surprise, by an escort of three hundred fellow-citizens on horse to his ship sixteen miles down the river. He arrived at London on December 10,

1764, and again found lodging with Mrs. Stevenson, the mother of Mary Stevenson, later the wife of Dr. Hewson. Forgetting, if one can, the apparent ease with which he reconciled himself to a separation for ten years from home, wife, and kindred, there is no pleasanter episode to recall in Franklin's career than his relation with these kind people. His letters reveal a most affectionate goodwill on both sides, and abound in many playful allusions to the complete hold which the great man had on the Stevenson household. He always fitted easily into any situation. Whether at the court of France or as a lodger in a London boarding-house, he was wholly himself, unaffected by grandeur and undisturbed by simplicity.

The few months which he thought would end his business of the petition soon slipped away, and nothing was gained. Meanwhile he had joined with other colonial agents in unsuccessful efforts against the famous Stamp Act which George Grenville succeeded in passing through both Houses of Parliament in March, 1765. Franklin's philosophic temperament rose superior to moral and patriotic enthusiasm. On the field of action he was impressed by the futility of opposition and by that concentrated force which England has always been able to present when its mind is made up on any course. Feeling as he did, it was natural that Franklin, in whom the statesman was as yet subordinate to the philosopher, should look for the wisest way out of a difficulty which he believed to be unavoidable, and that he should lend himself to Grenville's pretty scheme of selecting "discreet and reputable" stamp distributors from the colonists themselves by naming John Hughes, a personal friend of his in Philadelphia, as one of these distributors. Had Franklin then been making the world his confessor, he might well have put this step down as an erratum. Not one, probably, of the gallant horse who saw him depart for England could now have been found to welcome him home. His very friends and even his family were in danger of the popular hatred. Of all who aided or seemed to aid the enforcement of the odious Act, Mrs. Franklin alone seems, Ajax-like, to have defied danger.

But Franklin was then too old, as he was always too wise, a man to care overmuch for surface agitations. If he missed the point on this matter, it was because he was on the wrong side of the Atlantic. Moderate, peaceful by nature, the one American who had a universal reputation which had to be respected, if it was not liked, he kept his own counsel and felt his way carefully. To Grenville succeeded the ineffectual Rockingham cabinet, and within a year the potent antagonism of Pitt was felt against the absurdity of taxing unrepresented subjects. Right or wrong as Pitt's appeal may have sounded to English consciences, the non-importation agreements, by which the colonies were learning to do without the manufactures of the mother-country and finding out in a measure their own domestic resources, were touching the English pocket, and that is a matter of life or death, not of ethics. Lacking one month of a year from the passage of the Act, Benjamin Franklin gave testimony as to its expediency. Not only was he equipped, as every witness should be, to stand the searching examination to which he with others was subjected, but he was absolutely master of the situation. It was another instance of the extraordinary opportunity which a provincial of supreme ability has sometimes to prove himself the compeer of the administration of a central government. "No, they will never submit to it," was his laconic but not impetuous answer to an obvious question. And then the culminating assertion that "the Parliament of Great Britain has not, never had, and of right never can have, without consent given either before or after, power to make laws of sufficient force to bind the subjects of America in any case whatsoever, and particularly in taxation."

It would be ridiculous to say that Franklin posed on this his first of several notable appearances in public. He must have realised, as a man of extraordinary discernment, that the situation was dramatic, and that the surroundings lent themselves to make an effective picture. There is a certain staginess in any deliberative Assembly, and Parliament was no exception. Perceiving this, as doubtless he did, his unerring sense may have told him that entire simplicity and candour best became the situation: that these qualities were innate only made his attitude the stronger. A few weeks later the Stamp Act was

BENJAMIN FRANKLIN 71

definitely repealed, as much to the joy of British exporters as of the colonists. If Franklin's reputation had sagged a little within the year, it rose at once to dizzy heights. Success makes the spirits bright, and even Franklin's complacency responded to the change in his fortunes. Some of his cleverest writings appeared at this period. It was his keenest pleasure to "jolly" his friends and now and then the public. The admirable dulness of the British mind was an inviting target for some of his sharpest barbs. Never malicious, he felt sure that his wit would not severely wound, and that there was a good chance that he would not be understood. It was hard for the English to comprehend the resources of America, when the colonists began to do without manufactures. Accordingly, Franklin informs his British readers that colonial sheep were so blessed by nature that each "has a little car or wagon on four little wheels" to keep its wool from dragging on the ground. In the same skit he tells of the plans in operation for a cod and whale fishery in the "Upper Lakes," where the cod fly for safety from their huge foe. "The grand leap of the whale in the chase up the Falls of Niagara is esteemed by all who have seen it as one of the finest spectacles in nature." His *Rules for Reducing a Great Empire to a Small One* even Swift might have been glad to father, though it was lacking in the great satirist's intensive scorn.

Thus writing to please himself and perhaps others, unusually honoured in England and in France, and intrusted now with the agencies of New Jersey, Georgia, and Massachusetts, the next few years passed on still finding Franklin in what seemed the home of his adoption. He speaks hopefully in his letters of returning home, but still he lingers, till at last he does not pretend even to himself that he is on the eve of departure.

If Benjamin Franklin was devotedly attached to the land of his birth, he was also true to the country which seemed at that time to have adopted him. No important word of Franklin exists which tends to show that he cherished the idea of separation so long as cohesion was a possibility. Shelburne's ministry could not have been displeasing to him, for it was the creation of the friendly Pitt, and there is no telling what in the way of reconciliation might have come to pass, had it not been for Charles Townshend, Shelburne's chancellor of the exchequer. Townshend was cursed by the audacity of brilliant parts, which is even farther from the condition of supreme ability than is an honourable and commendable stupidity. His galloping career was cut short by death in the fall of 1767, and three months later Lord Hillsborough succeeded Shelburne as secretary of state for America. Franklin had a marvellous capacity for "getting along" with men, but he had a latent impatience for routinists and dryasdusts. Hillsborough was not to his liking, and he showed it. As a result, the new secretary, piqued by Franklin's acid retorts, refused to recognise the American as agent for Massachusetts, though he had been appointed by a vote of the House of Representatives of that province. Shortly after Franklin had the pleasure of causing the resignation of Hillsborough, who in the Board of Trade opposed him and others in the matter of the Walpole Grant (the grant of a tract of land on the Ohio River to a company of which Thomas Walpole, a London banker, was president). To Hillsborough's inadequate objections, which read absurdly to-day and may have read so then, Franklin in turn presented a reply to the Privy Council, who voted down the noble lord, whom Lord Dartmouth succeeded in August, 1773. Dartmouth was a good man, and not unfriendly to the now recognised Massachusetts agent, but the exigencies of politics are severe. In a few months occurred one of those dramatic events which make Franklin's career appear so vivid,— the famous episode which inflicted great damage on Franklin's immediate reputation and peace of mind, but which involved him inextricably on the American side, while he was yet sanely and moderately trying to play the part of reconciler.

The story of the "Hutchinson Letters," like many another event of history, is none the worse for an air of mystery which even now surrounds it. The fate of empires did not hang on its issue, but there were some uncomfortable moments for Benjamin Franklin before the tale was finally told. Here it must be rehearsed with the greatest brevity.

It was common opinion that the English government acted wholly on its own knowledge and prejudice in its stern and irritating attitude toward the colonies, and in particular toward the town of Boston. Franklin held this opinion, and expressed it freely. An Englishman, whose name is still unknown, told him that such severities resulted from information and advice proffered by certain Americans, and corroborated his assertion by placing in Franklin's hands a batch of indisputably authentic letters written by Governor Thomas Hutchinson, Lieutenant-Governor Andrew Oliver, and three others, every one of them native-born residents of Massachusetts Bay. To-day we may think of these gentlemen—for gentlemen they surely were—as Royalists, Loyalists, Tories, Traitors, anything we please to consider them; but in their own times they were flesh of our flesh, and not thought of as aliens, unpopular as they may have been. What these colonial bureaucrats wrote "home" about the doings of the rebellious people whom they governed was calculated to affect the people of Boston then very much as the pamphleteering work of Anti-imperialists in the same town in modern days affected the American spirit in the West. It was just simple treason. Franklin hoped or — shall we dare to say? — pretended to hope that the violent feeling of the colonists against England would be modified, could they realise that the mother-country had acted on the advice of some of their own leaders. Accordingly, under a strict injunction that the letters should not be printed or have a public circulation, he gained permission to send them to Massachusetts. They reached the hands of Thomas Cushing, then speaker of the House of Representatives. In some fashion, dishonourable, but explicable in those heated times, they found too speedy a publicity, and were ordered to be printed by the Assembly in express violation of Franklin's injunction. The letters created all the excitement to be expected, but not a whit of that abatement of hostility to England for which Franklin had looked; only a rage against the respectable writers, who in turn were angry enough that the privacy of their correspondence was thus violated.

Franklin as transmitter of the letters was still undiscovered, but it was an easy matter in England to learn that the addressee was William Whately, once private secretary of Grenville. Whately was dead, and his papers had been violated. Who did it? Thomas Whately, executor of his brother's estate, and John Temple were suspected. "Jack" Temple, Governor Bowdoin's son-in-law, was something of a blade and hot-headed. He demanded that Thomas Whately should assert positively that he, Temple, had never misused his brother's letters, to which he admitted he had had recourse. This Whately was unable to do, and, therefore, the two men, once friends, fought with pistols. Their blood was up and was Saxon, not Gallic. Consequently, they failed to see the lighter side of such an encounter, which was not without its amenities, though Whately was badly wounded. At this point, hoping to stay further bloodshed, Franklin on December 23, 1773, admitted over his own signature in the press that it was he, as the Massachusetts agent, who obtained and sent the letters to Boston. He completely exonerated both Whately and Temple from the least complicity in the affair. In August Franklin had placed before Lord Dartmouth the petition to the king from the Massachusetts House, praying the removal of Hutchinson and Oliver, but had heard nothing of it. If Franklin in this matter was not representative of the conscience of the colonists, he certainly embodied their audacity and spirit of resistance, or what we should now call their "nerve."

Here was a chance to put his courage to a test, and he was accordingly summoned early in January, 1774, to appear before the Committee for Plantation Affairs. On that occasion he presented to the committee the petition, with copies of the papers in the case, and asked for an adjournment, that he might secure counsel. On January 29 hearing was reopened in the Committee Room of the Privy Council, known as the Cockpit. His counsel, John Dunning and John Lee, proved ineffective, and Franklin was forced to bear alone the terrific assault of Alexander Wedderburn, afterward Lord Loughborough, counsel for Hutchinson and Oliver. Invective and personal abuse were carried to their highest point by Wedderburn, and these Franklin bore with consummate dignity. He would not, however, reveal the means by which he gained possession of the papers. Repine as we may over the question of political ethics, it is nevertheless true that in statesmanship and diplomacy a man may side with his cause. It is possible to accuse Franklin of personal indelicacy in sending the famous letters to Massachusetts, but in doing so he acted, precipitately, no doubt, as if he were representing the powers of a state in time of war to employ unusual means to uncover the plans of the enemy. His refusal to betray a personal trust, by refusing to tell how he gained possession of these papers, was the offset to the other part of the transaction. But nothing could save him from speedy punishment. His years of mediation between the colonies and the mother-country, the respect in which he had been so generally held in England, counted him nothing. The coarse abuse of Wedderburn, a man of mean repute, whose career was even then degenerating, expressed well enough a rising sentiment against the already disgraced colonial agent. Later he was dismissed from the postmaster-generalship of America.

XI.

As often happens, when personal abuse is used instead of calm dissection of facts, the victim of such abuse is the gainer. Wedderburn thought, in that famous scene in the Cockpit, to destroy utterly the reputation and standing of the old colonial agent, but he went too far. Those in England who were true to Franklin became still more true. Many of them remained his friends during the Revolution.

His conciliatory sentiments are now rapidly disappearing. In a fortnight he writes to Thomas Cushing that he is at a loss to know how peace and union are to be maintained or restored between the different parts of the empire. Although he was able to say that he had "not lost a single friend on the occasion," he began to turn his thoughts homeward. In the time remaining to him in England he showed no depression of spirits, but busied himself, as usual, with all sorts of interests. He writes to Beccaria in Italy on the resistance of a vacuum to the passage of the electric fluid, and thinks that this discovery may ultimately give new light on the aurora borealis. To Condorcet he gives information, geological and palæontological, regarding parts of North America. He dines with clergymen, littérateurs, scientific men, politicians, statesmen, with all who made the life of his day more vivid and helpful to him. There were homely gifts from home to share with his friends and enjoy, perhaps first of all, himself. There were people to help by his advice, and undertakings of every sort to encourage by his friendly aid. Nor did he scorn to turn his grave attention to the rendering of decayed meat sweet by placing it in fixed air. Even the defence of marriage with a deceased wife's sister was not too remote to engage his busy mind. These and other activities served no doubt to soothe the irritating wound dealt him in the presence of his enemies. Certain it is that in the short year left he had little to say about healing the breach between England and her American colonies. He was in effect an Englishman no longer; and, when he sailed for home on March 20, 1775, his allegiance, nominal and real, practically ceased. Still there did linger in Franklin's pacific disposition a wish to do all that he possibly could to preserve the integrity of an imperial system in which he continued to believe until the last. Had it not been for the "blunderers," he foresaw a possible future in which "we might have gone on extending our Western Empire, adding Province to Province, as far as the South Sea."

While aboard Captain Osborne's "Pennsylvania Packet," bound home, Franklin addressed to his "dear son"— so soon to disappoint him bitterly by turning Loyalist — a long account of the negotiations in London for effecting a reconciliation. This circumstantial and sometimes tiresome narrative gives all that it is necessary to know of Franklin's last efforts to hold to the old moorings the new American ship of state, now straining to be free. His conferences with the Honourable Mrs. and Lord Howe and with the great Chatham are carefully set forth, but, since they all came to nothing, have left a less deep impression than many others of Franklin's writings. Fine company never "feazed" the easy-going colonial. Going to keep one of his appointments with Chatham, he was so absorbed in a new pamphlet that he was carried a mile beyond the statesman's gate. Yet, like Thackeray, he was not displeased with the intimacy with greatness, and admits to not a little vanity on the occasion of a visit from Chatham, at his unpretentious lodging at the Stevensons' on Craven Street, exactly a year to a day from the Cockpit episode. The unsuccessful negotiations will not live except in the careful memories of historians, but from them was born one memorable phrase, coined by the Earl of Chatham. When he presented on February 1, 1775, his "Provisional Act" for settling the troubles of America, he referred to Franklin, with whom he had closely consulted on the provisions of this Act, as "an honour not to the English nation only, but to human nature," and meant it to be a deliberate reply to the disdainful looks and sayings of the blundering majority directed against the American commoner as he leaned against the bar in the Cockpit.

What the incomparable Pitt could not effect was certainly too hard a problem for the well-meaning Howe and his sister. All that remained of their endeavours is this statement of Franklin, who proves by it that he had done his best to the latest moment to avert what was bound to happen.

The battle of Lexington had been fought a little over a fortnight before the 5th of May, when Franklin came home. His wife had been dead five months, but the house in which she had faithfully carried out all the directions of her husband awaited him. The unabated cheerfulness with which Franklin managed to live for many years away from the company of his good wife may easily give rise to all sorts of surmises. He sent her many choice gifts and sums, not too frequent, and now and then moderately ardent letters. He asked and seemed to wish sincerely to have her join him in England, but she felt the usual terrors of the uneducated for untried experiences, and refused to cross the Atlantic. So he remained in great contentment away from her, and she stayed at home, carrying out his behests as carefully as she could. He grew stronger in power and influence and mental equipment every day: she stayed where she was put, dutiful, but unprogressive. He was a consummate master of the use of his pen: she was terribly illiterate, even for those days. In 1784, when he was again taking up the writing of his Autobiography, which he meant for the eyes of all men, he paid high tribute to his young wife, of whom he says, "It was lucky for me that I had one as much disposed to industry and frugality as myself." But, writing to her when she was an old woman, three years before her death, when she had already begun to fail in mind and body, though perhaps he did not realise the fact, he, in unloving phrase, tells her that she was "not very attentive to money matters" in her "best days," and practically orders her not to go about among his friends to borrow money. His harshness may have been necessary, but it is a sufficient rev-

BENJAMIN FRANKLIN

elation of that masculine cruelty whi smiles abroad and wears a hard face home. Probably Deborah Franklin, li many another simple-hearted wife, co doned such things as the foibles greatness.

XII.

IF Franklin felt for a moment the loneliness of age on his return to Philadelphia, he was not allowed to cherish it, for within a day from his arrival he was made one of the three deputies from the Assembly to the Continental Congress, which met on May 10. As chairman of the Committee of Safety for the province, an office which he held for eight months, the old man was presiding from six to nine in the morning; then went to the sittings of Congress until four o'clock in the afternoon.

As if serving on ten committees were not enough for his nearly seventy years, he accepted the office of Postmaster-General. Dismissed in disgrace as a deputy by his mother-country, in a little more than a year he was asked by the new country to give to the highest position possible to him the full benefit of his years of experience in post-offices, and was able to lay sure and lasting foundations for this important branch of government. If he was fond of revenge, Benjamin Franklin often had a chance to indulge a sweet tooth. As years before he had also learned something of the nature of preparation for service in the field and had mobilised the Pennsylvania forces in an efficient manner, so now he addressed himself to the task of making ready for a longer fight. Perhaps Washington, with whom he conferred on the general military condition at Cambridge camp in October, 1775, remembered how Franklin had raised in an incredibly short time that baggage train of one hundred and fifty wagons and pack-horses for Braddock's expedition just twenty years before. It is easy to forget amid the general splendour of Franklin's career or careers, as we may justly say, that he made a respectable record as a soldier. When Governor Morris commissioned him to take charge of the north-western frontier, he actually had nearly six hundred men under him in service, and deserved, according to the words of a contemporary, "a statue for his prudence, justice, humanity, and above all for his patience." It is fair to assume, then, that to Colonel, if not to Postmaster-General Franklin, General Washington gave a listening ear in those tentative days in the camp before Boston.

The greatest and most exacting period of Franklin's life was soon to open, but before he actually entered the field of high diplomacy he had one more direct service to render his country on this continent. It has always been a dream of continental largeness and vagueness — perhaps not yet wholly dissipated — that Canada and the United States might in some way "get together." That such an idea should gain strength among the revolting colonies was most natural, however slender the basis for any hopes that Canada — always the more provincial of the two great British possessions—would disavow allegiance. However all this may have been, a commission was appointed in 1776 to go to Montreal and make the necessary overtures. Samuel Chase, Benjamin Franklin, and Charles Carroll, the signer, were this commission, and with them went John Carroll, later Roman Catholic archbishop of Baltimore. According to Franklin's own account the journey was a hard one, and the result unsuccessful. No money could be borrowed, and no enthusiasm for separation was discoverable. Franklin's health was injured in this exposure to a northern spring, but he found a good friend in John Carroll, whom he afterward had the pleasure of naming as the best man for an American Roman Catholic bishop.

Back in Philadelphia by June, he was in season to be chosen a delegate from that town to a convention for the formation of a constitution. He was one of the five who drafted the Declaration of Independence, and was elected on July 8 as president of this Constitutional Convention, which chose him within two weeks as a member of the Continental Congress. Notwithstanding that he had sat in a body which had just renounced allegiance to the King of England, Franklin still found it consistent with patriotism and in harmony with his fondness for all peaceful measures, when they were possible, to accept a position on the committee appointed by Congress, consisting of John Adams, Edward Rutledge and himself, to listen, but hardly more than that, to the two brothers, Lord and General William Howe, who composed a commission of reconciliation. It may be that Franklin hoped that such a conference would bear more fruit than the numerous meetings with the Howe family in London, but, if so, his hopes were in vain. Beyond a courteous reception and good fare of cold ham, mutton, claret, and other substantial things, the Americans gained nothing from this meeting in the Staten Island house to convince them that these joint commissioners had authority large enough to deal with the important issues before them. No one has ever doubted the sincerity of purpose or the good-will of these brothers; but they were in this fruitless interview at the mercy of far abler men, and they lacked the capacity for settling a problem, so far advanced toward war, by the higher methods of diplomacy.

With the last hope of mediation gone and the Declaration of Independence promulgated to do its effective work, Congress had to face directly the practical side of revolution. So far the colonies had had sufficient vitality to resist small and irregular efforts to maintain the British authority. Skirmish had been well met with skirmish, but all was sporadic, and the Americans were favoured by good fortune. The actual resources of England had not been tested in any way. Money and European assistance were naturally the first things to be thought of. Three countries were actively hostile to the mother-country, and France was the most important of these three. France had lost her possessions in North America a quarter of a century before, but her feelings in the matter were chargeable to England rather than to the colonies. What had been wrested from her now remained loyal. There was, therefore, no especial hostility to the American cause; so far as it could be perceived, "revanche" then played no part in the sentiments of the French. But they were watchful and had their plans, it would seem, tentatively formed before Congress had begun to turn hopefully to Louis XVI. and his ministers.

XIII.

No one need look, even in the great Diplomatic Correspondence of the Revolution, for sentimental yearnings on the part of these astute French managers of statecraft to assist disinterestedly a struggling group of colonies in rebellion against a common foe. The situation was a perfectly cold-blooded one which faced the three commissioners, Benjamin Franklin, Arthur Lee, and Silas Deane, appointed later in 1776, to secure the powerful aid of France. Franklin, a month before he was seventy-one years of age, arrived at Nantes, used up by the second hard experience of travel within a twelvemonth. Well might Lord Stormont, the British ambassador, whom Franklin so unmercifully bull-baited in the immediate future, write, when he heard of his arrival, that he looked upon him as a "dangerous engine," for Franklin ere long was able to put the noble lord in a ridiculous position by a *mot*. It was clear to no one just why Franklin had come to France. Some thought that he was running away from a cause soon to collapse, some that he might eventually begin to negotiate with England; and, naturally, the majority took the obvious view that he was seeking in some form the support of France for the American cause. There was no doubt whatever about the sensation that he made. It was impossible for the English not to admire such a display of their favourite virtue, manly courage. The French, like the Gauls of old, "itching for novelties," as Cæsar found them, welcomed him as a great curiosity, not forgetting his reputation, already established among them, as a man of science and a philosopher.

He became at once so much the "man of the hour" that, in self-protection, he was obliged to retreat to Passy, which remained his headquarters during his mission. There he planned and transacted his diplomatic work, there he wrote his innumerable letters, among them tender messages to charming women, with whom he found time to play the harmless but assiduous gallant, to the disgust of the Adamses and the frenzy of Arthur Lee. He even found or made time to return to his early trade of printing, and in his Passy house set up a press, cast types, and printed various *jeux d'esprit* which he distributed to his friends. He brought this plant and the fonts of type to America, not without considerable trouble, and with this material set up in business his grandson, Benjamin Franklin Bache, later the editor of the *Aurora* and a chief calumniator of Washington, who established, or rather disestablished, Bache's social standing by refusing to receive him.

Seemingly, he was a man of large leisure with an opportunity for doing many little things. It is a not uncommon trait in ability such as his to work much harder out of sight than when in the public gaze. Charming as was the effect which he produced by his *bonhomie* and his leisurely effect on a nervous race, the errand on which he and his associates were bent was serious in all conscience,—literally, a "gamble" for a continent. By the last of December, 1776, they had audience with the Count de Vergennes, minister for foreign affairs. Their credentials were received, and their wishes for a treaty of amity and commerce pressingly stated. Their memorial to Gérard de Rayneval, secretary of the foreign office, presented soon after, was met with some indirection, certainly with no assurances of aid. It was something, however, to secure two million francs to be repaid without interest, when the American government was in a condition to pay its debts. So far, so good. But Vergennes, however friendly his intentions, was in no position to give open offence to Lord Stormont or his government. Stormont's policy was to prevent vessels destined for America, and often loaded with important and necessary cargoes for carrying on the various requirements of war, from clearing from French ports. A large portion of the impressive volumes of facsimiles so patriotically edited by the late Henry Stevens is taken up with the correspondence occasioned by these harassing delays. The French government was powerless to take a positive stand in regard to this holding up of outward bound vessels, and Stormont pressed the advantage of his position to the fullest. The American commissioners meanwhile were literally besieged by spies, their mails were opened, in London, and even in Paris. Franklin knew, or at least admitted it as a possibility, that his own secretary, Dr. Edward Bancroft, was betraying information; but nothing disturbed his equanimity, although it was necessary for the French police to safeguard the "respectable old man" from possible assassination.

The correspondence and daily business of these commissioners was, we may well believe, exacting to the last degree. There was no corps of young attachés to which much detail might have advisedly been intrusted, no busy little army of stenographers and typewriters capable of turning off finished pages almost as soon as the words were uttered. Everything had to be done with the care and precision which characterised the dignified processes of diplomacy of the eighteenth century. It was painful work, but it remains a credit to American political ability and method. The sailing-masters of the little fleet of American vessels had to be instructed, warned, placated. They, too, were harried by British spies, who caught them by the sticky lime of dissipation, always dear to the easy-going sailor-man, and to be enjoyed at its gayest in *la belle France.* Perhaps one of the hardest tasks which befell Franklin was that of cooling down gently, yet decisively, the large military aspirations of young Frenchmen, many of them of important lineage and position, but some of them adventurers pure and simple. The record of military service rendered this country by gallant French officers is so brilliant that we may be forgiven a smile when we reflect what would have been the effect on our army, our commissariat, and our military chest, had all the aspiring geniuses who sought to rid America of Britain's chains found their way here. But Franklin was equal to occasions such as these, and, though sorely tried by their applications,—supplications they often were,—managed to convey his refusal without giving offence. Some of his letters to applicants are marvels of polite ingenuity.

More important than the demands of

ravening sea-dogs, some of whom proved to be arrant knaves or insolently insubordinate, or than the importunity of aspirants for glory beyond-sea, was the need of securing the assistance of other European countries. Franklin had absorbed so much of the attention of the French people that a way to gratify the ambition of the other American diplomats fortunately opened toward other fields of diplomacy. Arthur Lee, already furiously jealous and suspicious of Franklin, essayed to interest Spain and Russia in our fortunes, but without success. Carmichael failed at the outset to attract Sweden, while John Adams later went to Holland, Francis Dana to Russia, Izard to Tuscany. None of them successfully influenced these various countries, and France remained through the war the true diplomatic stamping-ground.

There was not so much talk about "republican simplicity" as there was later when our government was at last a going concern, with the Federalist machinery running and the Republicans filled with dread, real or assumed, of aristocratic tendencies in our official life. We were not wholly free from monarchical habits of good living in high life, and our representatives in Europe, especially in Paris, lived comfortably. Although Franklin's style, according to Vergennes, was "modest," he spent about fifteen thousand dollars a year. He drew, however, in a recorded fifteen months only a trifle over twelve thousand dollars. It is more than one hundred and thirty years since this time when Franklin and those about him accomplished much because they set up no eccentric and novel standards of living in the midst of a well-established civilisation; yet to this day this country has never settled to its own satisfaction whether its foreign representatives should set a peculiar social pace or follow that which is found awaiting them.

These matters did not trouble Franklin, for he drew upon his own reasonably large fortune, and in respect to unselfishness of this sort was as nobly patriotic as Washington himself. According to Albert H. Smyth, he discharged the "varied duties of merchant, consul, commissioner, and plenipotentiary," subject all the while to drafts from Congress upon loans which it was assumed that he had made from the French government. He seems to have paid his personal secretary, his grandson William Temple Franklin, out of his own purse, for making copies of and caring for the vast correspondence incidental to his labours, a sum which at no time reached over fifteen hundred dollars a year. To the day of his death he had pleaded in vain for a settlement of the accounts between him and the government, which he literally carried on his back for nine years. Had Benjamin Franklin rendered no other service to his country or shown ability in no other way, his financial services to the United States would entitle him to gratitude too large ever to be fully repaid. That the government was at its wits' end for money is only an explanation, hardly an excuse. Any one but a Franklin would have been driven to madness by the exactions made upon him by Congress, through the reluctant Morris, but, since he was Benjamin Franklin, he shouldered through the mess. Perhaps that carelessness and lack of order against which he had striven — on paper — early in life, by means of binding "rules of conduct," and of which he was insultingly accused by Arthur Lee, and even by the honourable but fussy John Adams, may have saved him from final despair. What he could not perform, he let go, like the wise man he was. But, if he was accused of slovenly methods of routine, no charge of personal gain can be made against him. He had boundless opportunity to enrich himself,—vast sums passed through his hands, possible commissions were spread before his eyes. Able Americans since his day, men without a fraction of his commercial and money-getting genius, have fallen victims to temptations less alluring. But Franklin's record is white, although he made no loud pretences to austerity and even took a tolerant view of the adventurings of Silas Deane, and probably was more amused than scandalised at that political histrion, the lively and audacious Beaumarchais and his little, mysterious banking house of Hortalez et Cie. Job-like, he found his associates, nominally his friends, more trying or elusive even than his open enemies. Only on the rarest occasion did he lift his voice or use his pen against any of them, and then with a display of serenest dignity.

XIV.

It is difficult to tell the complicated tale of Franklin in France. There were many chapters, and the threads of narrative run in many directions. It is not necessary to disentangle these threads or to make continuity out of confusion. The main object of the commissioners was to secure an effectual treaty of amity and commerce, and then of alliance for mutual defence. Lord Stormont's object was to prevent such plans, and it was the part of Vergennes to be gracious to America and make no open breach, at least not yet, with England. So at first matters went on,—things do not drag in Paris,—the situation growing tenser, and harder for the commissioners than for any one else. To their surprise came a sudden and happy conclusion for the anxious envoys. The French were full of enthusiasm for the "insurgents," but, in spite of Franklin's efforts, had no disposition to put money into the American Revolution as an investment. Vergennes, forced by Stormont, moved rather threateningly against the violations of the neutrality laws by privateers, which were actually hurrying prizes out of French ports. This statesman even felt obliged to oppose the publication of Dubourg's translation, made at the instance of Franklin, of our various State constitutions. The public meanwhile, in cafés and in the streets, grew hotter and hotter, so far as zeal counts, for the American cause, and in the centre of all the tumult was the picturesque figure of an old man of simple garb, benign of countenance, spectacled and fur-capped, a true *homme du peuple*, yet withal a cool and calculating manipulator of great destinies.

But under all this froth there was a good brew. Enthusiasm had a substantial basis. Washington's capture of the Hessians at Trenton in December, 1776,

BENJAMIN FRANKLIN 111

and the defeat of the British at Princeton a few days later, gave joy in Paris, but it was not comparable to that caused by the news of Burgoyne's surrender at Saratoga on October 17, 1777. The official news reached the French government on December 4. Twelve days later the commissioners were told that the independence of America would be recognised, and that the treaties would be made. These treaties were signed on February 6, 1778, and the envoys, who up to this time were recognised only as private citizens, were received at court and this diplomatic achievement made public. No wonder that a British spy wrote that Doctor Franklin "is all life and full of spirits," though he did not fail to add defiantly, if illiterately, "possiably his course may be stopped shortly." The old man, in plainest but most decorous attire, no wig upon his venerable head, no buckles on his shoes, no sword at his side, was received as American commissioner, in mid-March, at the court of Louis XVI. A month later the Comte d'Estaing had sailed with the French fleet for America. Not France alone, but England, experienced the crisis caused by Burgoyne's surrender. The party of peace, never despicable in size or importance, grew in strength at this time. Franklin was in continual correspondence from this time on with such men as David Hartley and Dr. John Fothergill,—old associates in higher matters than the killing of human beings, and grave, determined lovers of peace. It was the natural object of these and other noble-minded Englishmen to discover a plan for ending the war without abasing England. Franklin was as humane as they, but entertained no project which did not involve a consideration of America's independence. That to him was already an accomplished fact.

It was John Adams who brought prim order out of annoying, even ridiculous chaos, when he supplanted Silas Deane who had been recalled by Congress, and who advised that Franklin be made sole plenipotentiary to France.

Though there was still an incredible amount to do, the business was practically now in Franklin's hands, and he was free to have his table littered and his papers in disorder, if he so chose to have them. Things went better, although they went none too easily. He could, however, look about him a little and draw a long breath when he wished. He was still the rage,—no man who ever lived was ever more so. The various biographies are full of this extraordinary popularity, which extended to every article of his attire and to his personal peculiarities.

It is impossible to write of the endless enthusiasm for everything he did or was without going over again one or another well-beaten biographical trail. Not only were there put on the market Franklin snuff-boxes, stoves, portraits, busts, common articles of ornament or use, but he himself was honoured by election to learned societies, chief among them the *Académie des Sciences*, as a foreign associate. Italy, Spain, Russia, honoured him greatly, but always as a man of science, as a philosopher, not as a statecraftsman. It is impossible not to suppose that Franklin was delighted at all this homage,—from the passing, frivolous sort, gone in an hour, had he made a political misstep, to the graver sort which recognised in him the embodiment of the spirit of the age in science and progress and of the new republican genius over seas. What wonder is it that the man who made a phrase (*ça ira*) that lived through a wilder revolution than our own, uttered in hours of discouragement to put new life into our cause, —what wonder is it that, buoyant, hopeful, though old in years, he failed in prophetic instinct, and had no perceptions of the hideous commotions underground to break out only ten years later! He was not a young man to see visions, but for an old man he dreamed few dreams of the past, and lived intensely in a vivid and engrossing present. To say that his head was turned by all this adulation would be to fail utterly to understand the composition of that head, as well balanced and composed a structure as ever surmounted a human body.

The one thorn in Franklin's complacent frame at this period was John Adams, who returned to Europe almost a year and a half after Franklin had been left in sole charge in Paris. He, too, was a great man, and great men oftentimes cannot sleep in the same bed, especially in political life. Fortunately, these two at heart each had an enormous respect for the other's main purposes. In the sifting process of history these differences amount to little more than this, that Franklin thought that Adams was too fussy, and the latter thought that his compeer was not fussy enough. Both were undoubtedly right, — certainly no part of the cause they served so gloriously was in the least injured by their differing attitudes.

The main object of his presence in France Franklin never suffered to be turned aside by such minor distractions as the quarrels of the captains, the importunities of adventurers, or the humiliating opposition of such men as Izard and the Lees. He was there to raise money to prosecute the war and to make the Declaration of Independence a living force. In all, up to 1783, he had secured from the French government 18,000,000 *livres*, to be paid finally by 1798; 10,000,000 *livres tournois* obtained in Holland, for which the French king made himself responsible; and, lastly, 9,000,000 *livres tournois* as "gratuitous assistance from the pure generosity of the King." Of this last gift, 1,000,000 *livres* were, so to speak, lost in transit from the Royal Treasury to the banking-house of M. Grand. It is a mystery not yet solved. Mr. Smyth says, "It has been traced to the doors of Beaumarchais's bank; beyond that point all knowledge of it ceases." Yet it was the fervid Beaumarchais, who, on hearing of the news of Burgoyne's surrender brought to France by Jonathan Loring Austin, made such haste to Paris and to Franklin that he nearly killed himself in a carriage,—a bearer of glad tidings, this buoyant, not scrupulous, yet by no means hateful gambler with destiny, Caron de Beaumarchais.

XV.

WITH the progress of American affairs, during his absence, no brief estimation of Franklin's career need have much to do. To astonish and enrapture France, while at the time he was gaining every point in financing the war,—that was his task, and it was after a while an accomplished fact. Meanwhile the Revolutionary cause was advancing, freshly energised by the needful sinews, the *livres tournois* so skilfully diverted into our empty chest. As our prospects brightened, the friends of peace in England waxed bolder, and the government's policy waned. There was rumour of the possibility of peace, tentative talks were held and messages written, but this basis for negotiations was unsound as long as the British clung to the vain hope of a reconciliation and sought to continue colonial dependence. There was another obstacle to progress in these irenic negotiations. It would be easy to concede much to America, could but the mother-country "avenge the faithless and insolent conduct of France."

No one understood better than Franklin how much was due to France or how scrupulously our obligations to her must be kept in any acts, diplomatic or otherwise, which pointed to a better understanding with England. A man as brilliant as Mr. Blaine might seem to forget such an agreement as the Clayton-Bulwer treaty, but it is impossible that Benjamin Franklin could forget the treaties of amity and commerce and alliance for mutual defence signed in February, 1778. He really loved and trusted France and even Vergennes as much as a wise and experienced old man could implicitly trust anything or anybody in a world so uncertain, even for an optimist. From an ardent lover of England, he had come to dislike and distrust her political methods, and what little hate there was in his ample nature was freely expressed for her arbitrariness. He never withheld his scorn from the amiable Hartley or from any of the various Englishmen who sought long for some accommodation by which peaceful measures might be considered.

It is a wholly unnecessary task to go into the least detail of the negotiations. They are, to say the truth, tiresome in the extreme, and, when intelligible, not in any way luminous. But they went on sporadically until Cornwallis gave it up at Yorktown in October, 1781. Even after that event, when North saw that "all was over," Franklin spurned the suggestion that England and America treat separately, without the partnership of France. The North ministry lasted five months longer. Richard Oswald, under the new Rockingham ministry, now enters on the scene, armed with good sense and reasonably full discretionary powers, but with no commission to treat.

The efforts of George Grenville to deal with France, and that meant with Vergennes, on somewhat parallel lines, may be neglected in this brief consideration. These efforts came to naught when the Shelburne ministry came in on the death of Rockingham. Oswald's powers were now increased. When at last he was enabled by his government to treat with the United States of America rather than with "Colonies or Plantations," matters began to go forward.

Then happened a strange thing. Jay and Adams were suspicious of the ultimate intentions of Vergennes, and doubted his ingenuousness in regard to American as contrasted with French interests. They believed that Franklin was in some way deceived. Franklin, on the other hand, was anxious to complete the business before Parliament met again, and finally yielded to his two fellow-commissioners. Parliament did not meet until December 5, 1782, and on November 30 preliminary and provisional articles were signed. Not until a treaty of peace had been executed between France and England was this treaty to be made definitive. The long and the short of it was that Franklin — for on him must the greatest responsibility rest — had negotiated with England alone without direct communication with the French court. It was his unpleasant task to inform Vergennes, as he did the next day, of the secret conclusion of the preliminary treaty, contrary to the definite instructions of Congress, and certainly contrary to the obligations implied and expressed which rested upon him personally to be open and loyal to Vergennes. The letter of the astute French statesman to Franklin was not a billet-doux, nor was Franklin's reply without a touch of over-explanation when no explanation ought to have been necessary. But the incident really went no further, and the definitive treaties between the three powers were signed on September 3, 1783. Strategically, the signing of the treaties with France in 1778 was the most significant act of Franklin's life, but his part in the treaty of peace was certainly the crowning act. Yet there was a fly in the ointment, and an uneasy sense of something wanting to make it a serene and perfect ceremony.

Vergennes in his letter to Luzerne, the French minister to the United States, accused Franklin of yielding "too easily to the bias of his colleagues," Jay and Adams, "who do not pretend to recognise the rules of courtesy in regard to us." He did so yield, but we may well believe not "too easily," and really against his own judgment. It were a long argument to defend or to attack Franklin successfully on this the great critical act of his career, one far more fraught with consequences than his publication of the Hutchinson-Oliver letters. In both cases he compromised something, — perhaps it was his personal honour. But successful statecraft seems unhappily to involve the necessity of compromise. The final answer to all discussion in this complicated problem will have to be that Franklin, through no fault or virtue of his, by yielding to the honest, irascible Adams and the courteous, upright, suspicious Jay, proved himself to have had some interior wisdom greater than his understanding, for it is beyond much peradventure that the two obstructionists to his desire for openness with France were mainly right in their fears and hesitations.

So practically were ended the great services abroad of the American plenipotentiary who during many years past had said and written with almost tiresome iteration that there was no good war and no bad peace. He remained in France to conclude commercial treaties with Sweden, Denmark, Portugal, Morocco, and lastly with Prussia to stop privateering.

XVI.

In spite of trying circumstances of many kinds, Franklin continued his life in Paris. The old friendly relations with individuals and with the whole people continued to the last. Born in Boston, where the holy zeal of the early days was passing and only the austerity remained, he seemed notwithstanding to have no trace of Puritanism in his marrow. John Adams, born much later, had enough for them both. Franklin, if we will but admit it, was really an Englishman, — a man of national, not colonial build. He was a Middle-States man by adoption, and assimilated easily the larger complacency of Pennsylvania ways. The worldliness of Parisian life troubled him as an old man as little as Boston Puritanism interested him when a boy. His orbit was large, and, above all things, he was not parochial. It is difficult not to believe that his intense affectation of a supposedly American dress, with its ultra-republican simplicity, was a harmless pose. However all this may be, he undoubtedly conversed enjoyably with philosophers and wits, saw life of every kind without being in the least affected unfavourably by extravagances. He ate good dinners and drank good liquors, in spite of his gout, of which he wrote as of a cherished friend. But, above all things, he liked the company of clever women, and they adored him.

Nothing in the life of any man can be more diverting or innocent than his letters to the daughter of Bishop Jonathan Shipley, to whom he wrote the famous epitaph on the squirrel, one of his cleverest *jeux d'esprit*, or to Mary Stevenson, at whose mother's house in Craven Street Franklin lodged so long and so happily when in London. His letters to Miss Stevenson are full of his best humour and good sense, yet these two friends could write on serious matters. In fact, this charming young lady had an astonishingly well-supplied mind, and was always ready to improve it. On these occasions the Doctor would reply as gravely as to a member of the Royal Society. In some of these Shipley and Stevenson letters Franklin appears to his best advantage as a sprightly, courteous gentleman of the world, never pedantic, never advancing too far in his sallies of robustious humour.

In his letters to French women, however, the spirit of gallantry is evident,— too evident for those who then and since had no relish for such epistolary chatterings. Had this disrelish not existed, it is improbable that the sixscore of letters written him by Madame Brillon, to whose daughter Franklin wished to marry his grandson William Temple Franklin, would have remained unpublished until Mr. Smyth gave us the best of them in the last volume of his definitive edition of the Works. The worst that one can say of Franklin in this whole matter is that toward that large and complicated subject known as the "ladies" he was soft. Some men do not like to be called *Cher Papa,* especially when they are old or getting to be so, but Franklin liked it. He spent much time, and doubtless much energy,—since tender letters are seldom spontaneous,—in communing with a woman who assures him that her "soul is pure, simple, frank." She was not simple, however frank, when she skilfully put aside Franklin's proposal that her daughter and his grandson should be married. To say that she was a French woman is to say that she was clever. If she was tantalising, she was also prudent. She tells him that no one loves him more than she does, but refuses him a treasure "which does not belong to me. I guard it and will always guard it carefully." There is abundant reason to suppose in glancing over these many letters, written in her extravagant humour and in Franklin's indifferent yet vivacions French, that the old man was not wholly satisfied to be "good Papa" to his *Chère fille*. Madame Brillon may not have bettered, though she did not lower, his ethical standards, but she did correct his French assiduously, and that is much to be grateful for when one is seventy-five. So verging sometimes, in their epistolary fashion, on the flowery edge of temptation, the French lady was always the more dainty in her risky steps, while "My Lord the Ambassador," as she calls him, treads at times heavily, even coarsely.

And there was Madame Helvétius of Auteuil, almost beloved of Franklin, and quite despised by Abigail, wife of John Adams. Sixty years had not taken away her power to charm, nor had they taught her to spell. Her letters lack the sparkle of Madame Brillon's, and are heavier with sentiment. She was a "kindly old soul," in the common parlance, and drew about her distinguished men of every sort,—men, however, who probably did not object to shine by contrast with their hostess; but Mrs. Adams thought her dirty. In one of his famous *jeux d'esprit*, the "Visit to the Elysian Fields," Franklin makes her the frankest sort of an offer of his hand, but in a *post-mortem* kind of way, for he imagines in the similitude of a dream, not in the choicest taste, that his wife and Helvétius have happily paired off, and so returns to earth and Madame Helvétius with the cry, "Let us avenge ourselves." But Mesdames Brillon and Helvétius were not anxious to ally themselves directly or indirectly to the house of Franklin, and remained only good friends to their American hero. There were other charming women to admire and be admired in France, but these two were first in his affections.

Mr. Smyth, in his rapid summary of Franklin's life which closes the definitive edition, draws a picture of Franklin sitting in his Philadelphia home on his return, attended by his "very gross and rather homely" daughter, visited by curious or homage-paying visitors, while his thoughts wander back to the pleasant land of France and the brilliant men and engaging women with whom he lived for years on such intimate and agreeable terms. One can but wonder whether the aged and fast dissolving philosopher contrasted his American home — and he always seemed to have loved a home in spite of his long and easily borne absences — with that gayer life. Did he ever smile grimly to himself at the strange, almost inexplicable misspelling of his daughter's married name which Madame Helvétius used in her letters, and wish that the prosperous old French lady had softened her heart, so that he might have ended his days in her agreeable company?

XVII.

In 1785 Franklin bethought himself of getting home. He was now in his eightieth year; his life-work was really done — so he thought — and he was in a feeble condition from the gout and gravel. Thomas Jefferson had been appointed his successor in March, and in May Franklin received the permission of Congress to return. The French king gave him a magnificent present, — a miniature of himself surrounded by a wreath of over four hundred diamonds, — a litter of the queen, drawn by mules, "who walk steadily and easily," was provided for the journey to Havre, — a necessarily slow journey because bodily disturbance gave him pain. There was a vast amount of baggage on which the English customs collected no duty. Arrived at Southampton from Havre, he went to the Isle of Wight. He saw some of his old English friends, and sailed from Cowes in a Philadelphia packet-boat, July 28, 1785. Among those who bade him farewell was his son, William Franklin, long alienated from his father by his espousal of the Loyalist cause. How sincere was the reconciliation no one can say: there was at least the outward aspect of paternal and filial decorum. Before he sailed, he visited Martin's salt-water hot bath and fell asleep in the water, on his back, watch in hand, and kept this position for nearly an hour. Did ever another philosopher in undress so utilise his time?

If there were wanting anything to attest the extraordinary nature of Franklin's ability, one fact would be enough. Experienced travellers, even in these days of comfortable going, agree that mental work at sea is impracticable and generally impossible. Yet this wonderful man spent the seven weeks of his voyage in writing memorable things, among them a treatise on smoky chimneys, another on the Gulf Stream and other maritime facts and problems, and yet a third on the burning of pit-coal. On Wednesday, September 14, on a flood-tide and a morning breeze he came in sight of "dear Philadelphia." "We landed at Market Street Wharf, where we were received by a crowd of people with huzzas, and accompanied with acclamations quite to my door. Found my family well. God be praised and thanked for all his Mercies!" Such was the homecoming of Benjamin Franklin, venerated, in spite of some discordant criticism which has lasted to this day, by two continents for reasons which appeal to the good sense and discernment of common humanity.

It was his expressed hope to be left in peace, but he had yet to receive many honours, chief among them the presidency of Pennsylvania. The American Philosophical Society, the University of Pennsylvania, and the Assembly of that

Commonwealth addressed him in a formal way. He was also a delegate to the Convention of States, convened in 1787, for deliberation on a National Constitution, and he attended the meetings faithfully, although walking was now difficult to him on account of his infirmities. There was truth in his remark made on his return, that his countrymen, having eaten his flesh, were resolved to pick his bones. But he probably liked the insistence on his remaining a public and active figure. His mind was still alert. He took the same interest in everything. Even a two-headed snake taken from the Schuylkill was not beneath his attention. Of greater import to him must have been the news of a "boat moved by a steam engine which rows itself against tide in our river." This was Fitch's invention, and he saw the possibilities of it, even stating it as his belief that it would "become generally useful," but even his far-reaching mind could not guess how useful. He met all happenings with his usual complacency. To his sister Jane, his favourite from early life, he wrote, "I have long been accustomed to receive more blame, as well as more praise, than I have deserved." But his two ancient foes, the gout and the gravel, of which he always spoke with ironical respect and with a real gratitude that they were not worse, were gaining on his years and his strength.

For the last two years of his life Franklin had withdrawn largely from public affairs and service, but continued to write letters and some papers of considerable though not the first importance. In 1789 he wrote his *Observations Relative to the Intentions of the Original Founders of the Academy in Philadelphia*, in which he brought forward with all his usual vigour his favourite theory that the English language should be taught "grammatically and as a language." While he did

not undervalue learning, he regarded—
and did not hesitate to say it—the teaching of Latin and Greek as equivalent to the habit of wearing the hat under the arm, long after the use of wigs had made the practice necessary; "the *chapeau bras* of modern literature" he called them. The annals of the leading American university for the past twenty years will show that this position taken by Franklin has, a hundred years later, grown to be a guiding principle,—first the English language, then the rest if you will. He was interested in the abolition of the slave-trade, and was president of the Pennsylvania Society for Promoting the Abolition of Slavery. His signing the memorial of the society presented to the National House of Representatives on February 12, 1789, was his last act of a public nature. On March 23 of the year, less than a month before his death, he sent to the *Federal Gazette* an ironical skit alleged to have been delivered by

Sidi Mehemet Ibrahim, of Algiers, in defence of slavery.

Small things as well as great still engaged his yet active intelligence. His zeal for good printing, good paper, good type, never died in him, though it must be said that he left no remarkable typographical monument as evidence of his faith. In fact, he was less fertile in device as a printer than in anything he achieved. In his trade he was really a conservative, and as late as 1789 was regretting the growing disuse of italic letters and of the long "s," comparing the monotonous effect thus produced to the paring of all men's noses smooth and level with their faces, though it rendered "their physiognomies less distinguishable." He disliked what he called "gray printing," and his letter of December, 1789, to Noah Webster tells him that the Philadelphia edition of his famous *American Spelling Book* is miserably printed and on "wretched paper." He always respected the usages of his craft, if he did not do much to better them. One flash of the old zeal for improving things is seen in his suggestion to put an interrogation at the beginning of a question instead of at the end.

On March 9, 1790, he wrote that famous letter to Ezra Stiles, president of Yale College, with whom existed a friendship of uncommon strength and mutual trust. In it he affirms nearly all of the religious faith which he was willing to profess, and it never suffers by repetition. Few philosophical minds of the eighteenth century went further, and most of them did not go so far. "Here," he says with memorable brevity, "is my creed." "I believe in one God, the creator of the universe. That he governs it by his Providence. That he ought to be worshipped. That the most acceptable service we render to him is doing good to his other children. That the soul of man is immortal, and will be treated with justice in another life respecting its conduct in this. These I take to be the fundamental points in all religion, and I regard them as you do in whatever sect I meet with them." He wrote in bed on March 24 to his sister Jane a cheerful letter for one in his condition, reiterating that, though his malady was severe, he could reflect with fortitude on how many more horrible evils the human body is subject to, and that he has been blessed with "a long life of health ... free from them all." The last letter he ever wrote was to Thomas Jefferson on April 8, recalling with perfect clearness his memory of the St. Croix River boundary and sending him a map of Passamaquoddy Bay.

Nine days later he died, on April 17, 1790, at the age of eighty-four years and three months. An aposteme, which had formed in the lungs, suddenly burst. His strength did not enable him sufficiently to throw off the discharge, and it is safe to say that septicæmia from the absorption of the remaining pus was the direct cause of the death. Whatever may be our view of the philosophy and the religion — if so we may call it — of Benjamin Franklin, there is no doubt whatever that they were steadfast aids to his composure as he neared and met his end. The nearest approach he made to a murmur at his pain were the words, reputed to have been his last, "A dying man can do nothing easy." By a curious turn of destiny this great apostle of good sense, this philosopher so free from whimsies and small prejudices, is supposed, if we may believe the words as recorded by John Adams of his attending physician, Dr. John Jones, to have succumbed neither to the gout nor the stone, but to a cold caught by sitting in the cold current coming through an open window. For half a century he had been proclaiming that colds were not caught simply by the coldness of the air, but by draughts, moisture, and other concomitants. This proves nothing of course except that, when one is nearly ninety, it is unwise to test too strongly the hypotheses of middle life. He was, however, a famous therapist, as well as a multitude of other excellent things, and deserves no ridicule because he fell a victim to his own empirical tests. His funeral and burial were as impressive as his life had been simple. Of the respect shown by persons, institutions, and political bodies every biography speaks at length. His memory was honoured in every possible way,— in public meeting, resolutions, addresses, and orations,— but in no way more signally than by the printers of Paris, who, on the occasion of a memorial meeting, caused to be set up, printed, and distributed to the audience the speech delivered by one of their number.

If the French printers thus signalised the one calling of which Franklin was most proud, he in his last will did not permit the fact to be forgotten, for this formal paper begins, "I, Benjamin Franklin, of Philadelphia, printer," and then goes on to say also, as if of secondary import, "late Minister Plenipotentiary from the United States of America to the Court of France, now President of the State of Pennsylvania." There is a slight but a sure ring of a commoner's defiance in thus putting occupation before office, or it may have been a harmless vanity to run up the *crescendo* of achievements. It was a famous will and carefully considered. No item therein contained is so well remembered as that relating to the sums devised to the cities of Boston and Philadelphia. These sums which were to have accrued according to his shrewd and authoritatively correct calculations have not turned out to be so large by a great deal as he thought they must, but they are respectably large. From the Boston fund has been established the worthy

Franklin Union with its trades-school and other practical aids to aspiring youth. On the large plate glass of a bank in Philadelphia many have seen the legend: "Estate of Benjamin Franklin. Estate of Stephen Girard." The potent influence of his life and of his honestly earned fortune still abides in a concrete and substantial way in the city of his adoption.

XVIII.

THE world — two worlds rather — have seen fit to ignore the defects of this most unusual man and to remember his virtues and his accomplishments as the qualities of few men, since history began, have been remembered. The minutiæ of his excellences are recalled. His witty sayings, his wise proverbs, are so familiar that they are part of the common mental inheritance of the race and are hardly now attributable to the author of them. Like the Bible and Shakespeare, his homely wisdom has lost its personal attribution. It is indeed a wonderful record. If one thinks of humble beginnings and great endings, one thinks of Franklin. The name occurs to every one who speaks of the dawn of electrical knowledge, of the growth of printing in this country, of the post-office system, of protection against fire, of early journalism, of the first successes in the publication of books, of the foundation of free libraries and free schools and colleges. In American art we must consider the innumerable busts, engravings, medals, paintings, and other attempts to preserve the features of this plain American. He ventured into the field of theology, philanthropy, philology, ethics, and even of military affairs. It would be a hard task to say whether he stands higher in reputation as a scientist or as a diplomat, for surely science and diplomacy have little in common, and few men have achieved greatness in both callings; yet it would be safe to say that he was pre-eminent in both. His own time thought so, and there is no reason to dispute the decision now.

BIBLIOGRAPHY

The few titles here given will amply serve as a guide to a reasonably full knowledge of Franklin's life and writings. A host of books have been written about him, many of them dealing with particular episodes of his career. Of his own writings many editions of no real consequence have appeared since the first issuance of his famous Autobiography. These editions generally contain this Life, some of his best-known essays, and almost without exception the famous *Way to Wealth*, which was a garnering of the more familiar sayings first incorporated in the *Poor Richard's Almanacs*. With the publication of John Bigelow's edition of the Life in 1874 begins the latest and only important knowledge of Franklin from a modern standpoint.

BIBLIOGRAPHY

BOGGESS, ARTHUR CLINTON, and EMMA REPPLIER WITMER. Calendar of the

Papers of Benjamin Franklin in the Library of the University of Pennsylvania. (Philadelphia, 1908.)

CALENDAR OF THE PAPERS OF BENJAMIN FRANKLIN in the Library of the American Philosophical Society. Edited by I. Minis Hays (Philadelphia, 1908. 5 vols.).

THE EXTRAORDINARY LIBRARY OF SAMUEL W. PENNYPACKER. Part I. To be sold, December 14, 1905. (Philadelphia, 1905.) Part I. contains books printed by Benjamin Franklin, books from the library of Benjamin Franklin, letters written by Benjamin Franklin and his son, William Franklin, etc.

FORD, PAUL LEICESTER. Franklin bibliography. A list of books written by or relating to Benjamin Franklin. (Brooklyn, N.Y., 1889.) Up to the time of his death Mr. Ford was an indefatigable student of Franklin and collector of Frankliniana. This bibliography still remains the best, although it is over twenty years old. Its immediate predecessor was the Catalogue of Works relating to Benjamin Franklin in the Boston Public Library, including the Collection given by Dr. Samuel Abbott Green. [Compiled by Lindsay Swift.]

UNITED STATES. LIBRARY OF CONGRESS. DIVISION OF MANUSCRIPTS. List of the Benjamin Franklin Papers in the Library of Congress. Compiled under the direction of Worthington C. Ford (Washington, 1905).

WORKS BY FRANKLIN

WORKS. . . . With notes and a life of the author. By Jared Sparks (Boston, 1836–40: Hilliard, Gray & Co. 10 vols.). This edition of Franklin's works superseded the edition in six volumes [Philadelphia, 1809–18, Duane], edited by his grandson, William Temple Franklin. It was in turn superseded by:

COMPLETE WORKS. . . . Compiled and edited by John Bigelow (New York,

1887–88: G. P. Putnam's Sons. 10 vols.).

WRITINGS. . . . Collected and edited with a life and introduction by Albert Henry Smyth (New York, 1905–07: The Macmillan Co. 10 vols.). This may safely be regarded as the definitive edition of Franklin's works and as taking the place of the Bigelow edition, sets of which have now grown scarce.

AUTOBIOGRAPHY. Edited from his manuscripts with notes and introduction by John Bigelow (Philadelphia, 1868: Lippincott & Co.). Later editions followed. Out of the great number of editions of the Autobiography this is the first in point of time which demands the attention of the modern reader. Afterward expanded into:

LIFE. . . . , written by himself. Now first edited from original manuscripts and from his printed correspondence and other writings by John Bigelow (Phila-

BIBLIOGRAPHY 151

delphia, 1874: Lippincott & Co. 3 vols.). A "fifth edition, enriched," was published in 1905.

AUTOBIOGRAPHY . . . , and a sketch of Franklin's life from the point where the Autobiography ends, drawn chiefly from his old letters. With notes and a chronological historical table. (Boston, [1896]: Houghton, Mifflin & Co. [Riverside Literature Series.]) An inexpensive and serviceable edition, quite good enough for ordinary use.

AUTOBIOGRAPHY. With an introduction by Woodrow Wilson. (New York, 1901: The Century Co. [The Century Classics.])

AUTOBIOGRAPHY OF BENJAMIN FRANKLIN. (Boston, 1906: Houghton, Mifflin & Co.) Beautifully printed, but without any especial distinction of editing. Franklin's life was told in homely fashion for plain people, and seems to require no splendid raiment to adorn it. Like a fine-looking man of toil, it appears to best advantage in workaday clothes.

POOR RICHARD'S ALMANAC and other papers. With notes. (Boston, 1886: Houghton, Mifflin & Co. [Riverside Literature Series.]) Serviceable and inexpensive, but not so useful as:

"THE SAYINGS OF POOR RICHARD." The prefaces, proverbs, and poems of Benjamin Franklin, originally printed in *Poor Richard's Almanac* from 1733–58. Collected and edited by Paul Leicester Ford (New York, 1890: G. P. Putnam's Sons [Knickerbocker Nuggets]).

SELECTIONS FROM THE WRITINGS OF BENJAMIN FRANKLIN. Edited by U. Waldo Cutler (New York [1905] : Crowell & Co. [Handy Volume Classics]). Contains a sketch of Franklin's life.

THE WISDOM OF BENJAMIN FRANKLIN: being reflections and observations of men and events, not included in *Poor Richard's Almanac*. Chosen from his collected papers, with introduction by John J. Murphy (New York, 1906: Brentano).

WORKS ABOUT FRANKLIN

FISHER, SYDNEY GEORGE. THE TRUE BENJAMIN FRANKLIN. (Philadelphia, 1899: J. B. Lippincott Co.)

FORD, PAUL LEICESTER. THE MANY-SIDED FRANKLIN. (New York, 1899: The Century Co.) If one were obliged to limit himself to the reading of a single work relating to Franklin,—excepting always the Autobiography,—Mr. Ford's book might surely be that one. He unearthed many hidden or stray facts, and combined them in a vivid and picturesque fashion.

HALE, EDWARD EVERETT, and EDWARD EVERETT HALE, JR. FRANKLIN IN FRANCE. From original documents, most of which are now published for the first time. (Boston, 1887–88: Roberts Brothers. 2 vols.)

MCMASTER, JOHN BACH. BENJAMIN

FRANKLIN AS A MAN OF LETTERS. (Boston, 1887: Houghton, Mifflin & Co. [American Men of Letters.]) Still holds its place as a satisfactory consideration of the literary side of Franklin's life, and a worthy companion to:

MORSE, JOHN TORREY, JR. BENJAMIN FRANKLIN. (Boston, 1889: Houghton, Mifflin & Co. [American Statesmen.]) Various later editions. A short, yet comprehensive account of Franklin's career, with emphasis on the political side.

MORE, PAUL ELMER. BENJAMIN FRANKLIN. (Boston, 1900: Houghton, Mifflin & Co. [Riverside Biographical Series.]) A compact account, showing an intimate and critical knowledge.

PARTON, JAMES. LIFE AND TIMES OF BENJAMIN FRANKLIN. (New York, 1864: Mason. 2 vols.) Lively and readable, like everything Parton wrote. A good appetiser for the more solid feast of the later estimates.